EDOARDO BONECHI

FLORENCE

A COMPLETE GUIDE FOR VISITING THE CITY

BONECHI - EDIZIONI « IL TURISMO »
FIRENZE

SERIE «MERCURIO»
DELLE GUIDE BONECHI

Translation by MERRY ORLING

© Copyright 1979 by BONECHI – EDIZIONI « IL TURISMO »
Via dei Rustici, 5 – 50122 FIRENZE – Tel. 298224/25

WELCOME TO FLORENCE

The first time you visit a city, your main objective is most likely to try to get a feel for its past and present while at the same time doing your best to spend as little time and money as possible. This, however, is not easy doing in the rare places like Florence that have left their mark on not just one, but on several periods of world history. Just how great an impact this city has had on civilization is borne out by the countless masterpieces turned out here in a continuous stream throughout the centuries.

In Florence a panoramic glance hardly suffices. A superficial look doesn't allow you to analyze and classify such incredible wealth of artistic and historical material and thus arrive at a deeper understanding of what you are seeing. I am delighted to fill the gap and introduce Florence to you with the aid of this book. Despite its compact size, it provides you with a thorough stone-by-stone description of the city that, starting from the Middle Ages and going up through this very day, has been the scene of such outstanding contributions to every branch of the arts and sciences. You will thus encounter Florence and learn to appreciate her unmistakable personality. The city will be revealed in contrasts — just as the stories you will read in these pages are full of contrasts, some brimming with joy while others tell of violence and hardship. I am sure that you will soon see my point. In the meantime, may I extend my warmest welcome to you and wish you a happy stay in Florence.

THE PUBLISHER

ITINERARIES

4

CONTENTS

5

FIRST ITINERARY

Piazza del Duomo (Baptistry of San Giovanni; Giotto's Belltower; Loggia del Bigallo; Cathedral of Santa Maria del Fiore; Cathedral Museum) - Medici-Riccardi Palace (Medici Museum) - Piazza San Lorenzo (Church of San Lorenzo, Laurentian Library, Medici Chapels).

Piazza del Duomo — This huge square, together with the adjoining Piazza San Giovanni surrounding the Baptistry, is the heart of Florence. The religious monuments to be found here — the Cathedral, the Baptistry, and Giotto's Belltower — create splendid harmony with their pink, green, and white marbles and geometric designs. By the Baptistry's north door is the so-called **Column of St. Zenobius,** put up here in 1384. It commemorates the miracle performed by the saint (who was bishop of Florence around the 5th century); an elm tree burst into flower as his coffin was being carried by in mid winter. Here every year on Easter Sunday the *"Scoppio del Carro"* (Explosion of the Cart), a traditional Florentine event, is held.

The "Scoppio del Carro" festival. The festival, whose origins are remote, is held every year on Easter Sunday at twelve noon sharp.

THE BAPTISTRY – One of the oldest buildings in the city, it was described as *"il mio bel San Giovanni"* ("my lovely San Giovanni") by Dante who was christened here in 1265. Originally it was thought to date back to the 5th century A.D., but now the general feeling is that the Baptistry was built in the Romanesque period (11th-12th centuries) over the ruins of an Early Christian structure (the foundation of which contains remains of an even earlier, Roman, construction). The exterior of the octagonal building, an outstanding example of the Tuscan Romanesque architectural style, consists of a two level arcade and a typically Romanesque green and white striped marble facing. The dome is hidden beneath an upper storey put up in the 13th century. The Baptistry was dedicated to St. John the Baptist and served as Florence's cathedral until the year 1128. The three portals on the north, south, and east sides are renowned as masterpieces in their own right.

Baptistry - Interior.

THE INTERIOR — It is better to look at the inside (generally the south portal serves as the entranceway) before examining the exterior. The eight-sided building has two levels, the lower one with Corinthian columns, the upper one with a narrow arched gallery. The walls are adorned with a geometric multicolored marble facing which is typical of the Florentine Romanesque style. The inlaid marble pavement of 1209 has zodiacal signs, and motifs which recall Oriental textiles. On the far side is a marble baptismal font, originally placed in the center of the building, which has six bas-relief panels (Pisan school, 1371). On the right wall is a famous Renaissance wall tomb by Donatello and Michelozzo (1427). It contains the mortal remains of the Antipope John XXIII who died in Florence in 1419. The triumphal arch of the apse and dome are aglow with 13th century Byzantine-style mosaics created by mastercrafts-men from Venice and Florence. The mosaics in the tribune were begun in 1225 by Jacopo da Torrita. Their subjects are: *Christ, Mary, Apostles, and Prophets,* and, in the double archway, the *Mystic Lamb with Patriarchs and Prophets*. In the center

9

Baptistry - The interior of the dome, entirely decorated with mosaics executed by Florentine and Venetian craftsmen from the second half of the 12th century to the beginning of the 14th century. The huge figure of Christ the Judge dominates the composition.

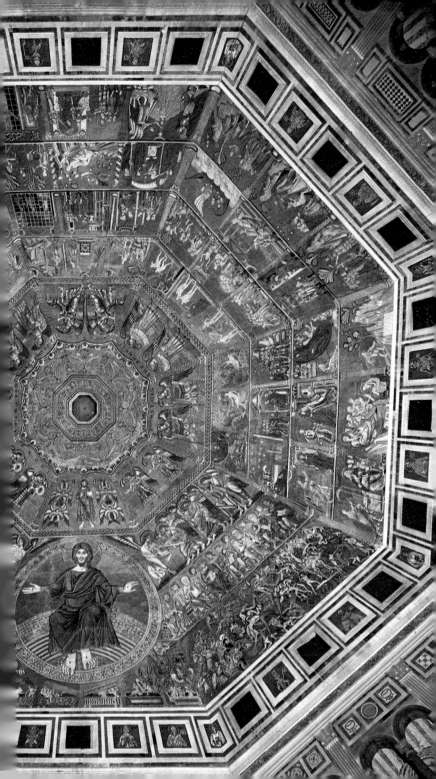

Baptistry - Andrea Pisano's South Portal.

of the ceiling are the *Virgin and Child* on the right, and *John the Baptist enthroned,* on the left. The marble candlestick holder in the shape of an angel to the left of the gallery is by Agostino di Jacopo (1320). The dome mosaics (which are lit up upon request) were made by Venetian and Florentine artists in the second half of the 13th and the beginning of the 14th centuries — Cimabue, Andrea di Riccio, known as Tafo, and Gaddo Gaddi. On three sides is a *Last Judgment* with a huge figure of Christ (over 26 feet tall). From top to bottom, the subjects in the registers are ornamental motifs, the *heavenly hierarchy,* the *story of Genesis,* the *story of Joseph the Jew,* the *story of Christ,* and the *story of John the Baptist.*

THE SOUTH PORTAL — This door created between 1330 and 1336 by Andrea Pisano is the oldest of the three. The casting was done by a Venetian, Leonardo D'Avanzo. The twenty-eight panels illustrate *scenes from the life of John the Baptist and allegories of the cardinal and theological virtues.* The doorpost decoration was sculpted by Vittorio Ghiberti, son of the famous Lorenzo Ghiberti, in 1462. The bronze statues above the portal depicting the Baptist, Salomé, and the Beheading of the Baptist are by Vincenzo Danti (1571).

THE NORTH PORTAL — This fine portal, often ignored by tourists who would never think of missing Ghiberti's more famous East Portal, is also by Ghiberti, who had the collaboration of Donatello, Paolo Uccello, Bernardo Ciuffagni, and Bernardo Cennini. The story of how the portal came into being is fascinating. In 1402 a competition for

Baptistry - Ghiberti's North Portal.

its design was announced, the theme selected being the Sacrifice of Isaac. Some of the most famous artists of the day submitted competition pieces — Ghiberti, Brunelleschi, Jacopo della Quercia, Nicolò Lamberti and many others. The Cathedral Committee judged the bas-reliefs submitted by Brunelleschi and Ghiberti as the two best—but finally awarded the commission to Ghiberti. The committee preferred Ghiberti's elegant composition and refined technique to Brunelleschi's more dramatic but less polished rendition. Modern judges might think differently—in any case, both models are exhibited in the Bargello where everyone may make up his own mind. The portal is divided into twenty-eight panels like the south door. The upper twenty illustrate New Testament scenes, the lower eight contain representations of the four Evangelists and Fathers of the Church. Ghiberti's style here is a mixture of Renaissance grace with naturalistic overtones. The same artist is responsible for the foliage, floral, and animal motifs framing the door. The three statues above, by G. Francesco Rustici (1506-1511), represent *Christ between the Levite and the Pharisee.*

THE EAST PORTAL — Opposite the Cathedral is this portal which Michelangelo supposedly called the "gate of paradise." It is considered the masterpiece of Lorenzo Ghiberti who worked on it from 1425 to 1452 — 27 years in all! He lavished all of his imagination and skill in designing and modeling these ten panels. Other well-known artists — Michelozzo, Benozzo Gozzoli, and Bernardo Cennini — also had a hand in executing the superb work. Recently restored, its original sheen of gilding is now visible. The iconographic scheme (Biblical subjects) was created by the famous humanist scholar, Leonardo Bruni, then Chancellor of the Republic.

13

Baptistry - Ghiberti's Gate of Paradise.

Creation of Adam and Eve. The Original Sin. The Expulsion from Paradise.

Adam and Eve with Cain and Abel. Abel shepherd, Cain ploughsman. Cain kills Abel. The curse on Cain.

Story of Noah - Noah's family leaves the Ark after the Flood. Noah thanks the Lord. The drunkenness of Noah. Noah derided by the son of Cam.

Story of Abraham - Sarah at the entrance to the tent. The angels appear to Abraham. The sacrifice of Isaac. The angel restrains Abraham.

Story of Jacob and Esau - Esau sells his birth-right to Jacob for a plate of lentils. Isaac blesses Jacob mistaking him for Esau. The departure of Jacob.

Story of Joseph - Joseph is sold to the merchants. The merchants present him to Pharaoh. Joseph interprets the Pharaoh's dreams. The golden goblet in Benjamin's sack.

Story of Moses - Moses receives the Tablets of the Law on Mount Sinai. The Israelites, terrorized by the thundering and lightening, wait at the foot of the mountain.

Story of Joshua - Joshua and the chosen people cross the Jordan which retreats before the Ark. The walls of Jericho fall at the sound of the angels' trumpeting.

Story of Saul and David - Saul defeats the Philistines. David kills Goliath. David triumphantly bears the head of the giant.

King Solomon ceremoniously receives the Queen of Sheba.

On the door frames Ghiberti alternated 24 statues of prophets and Sibyls with 24 medaillons of busts of artists, his contemporaries.

LEFT SIDE - Above, the reclining figure represents Spring. From top to bottom, on the left: the prophet Amos, the prophet Zechariah, the prophet Daniel; Judith, daughter of Jephtha. From top to bottom, right: the prophet Baruch, the prophet Elias, the Delphic Sibyl, the prophet Isaiah, the prophet Haggai. The reclining figure on the bottom represents Summer.

RIGHT SIDE - Above, the reclining figure represents Autumn. From top to bottom, left, the Tibertine Sibyl, the Persian Sibyl, the prophet Elisha, Joshua, the Cuman Sibyl. From top to bottom, right: Judas Maccabei, Samson, Jeremiah, Gideon, the prophet Ezekiel. At the bottom, the reclining figure represents Winter.

Lorenzo Ghiberti

Vittorio Ghiberti

The head in the middle of the door between the Delphic Sibyl and the prophet
Isaiah is a self-portrait of Lorenzo Ghiberti. The one between the prophets
Elisha and Joshua is a portrait of Lorenzo Ghiberti's step-father and teacher,
Bartoluccio. The fine doorpost with floral and animal motifs is also by
Ghiberti. On the architrave is a statue group of the "Baptism of Christ"
by Andrea Sansovino (1502). The Angel is by Innocenzo Spinazzi. On either
side of the door are red porphyry columns. They were captured from the
Saracens by the Pisans who then donated them to the Florentines as a
token of their gratitude for the Florentines' protection of their city while
the Pisan fleet was engaged in the Battle of the Balearic Islands.

The Loggia del Bigallo - *Right:* Giotto's Belltower.

GIOTTO'S BELLTOWER

GIOTTO'S BELLTOWER — Proudly soaring about 265 ft. into the sky, the tower is one of the most beautiful built by man. Shortly after Giotto, the great Florentine artist, was asked by the *Signoria* (the city's ruling body) to submit a design for a belltower, work got underway (July 1334). Unfortunately, Giotto died three years later, and never lived to see his project completed. A famed artist, Andrea Pisano, was then called in and he worked on the tower until 1348 when Francesco Talenti took over (Talenti finished the tower in 1359). Both Giotto's successors scrupulously stuck to the great master's plan with the exception of the crowning spire. The spire, which would have added another ninety-eight feet to the total height of the building, was never put up.

The Belltower is faced in colored marbles and decorated with superb bas-reliefs that are unequaled in all of Italy. The rectangular lower section is divided into two zones. In the lower one are relief panels by Andrea Pisano and Luca della Robbia (after designs by Giotto) which depict the *Labors of Man*. In the upper one are allegorical figures by Andrea Pisano and Andrea Orcagna. Above is the section designed by Francesco Talenti with sixteen niches that once contained statues by Donatello, Nanni di Bartolo, and others (they are now preserved in the nearby Cathedral Museum). The upper levels, pierced by graceful two and three-part windows, are topped by a cornice. Whoever climbs the 414 steps to the terrace is rewarded with a superb view of the city and the surrounding countryside.

The Loggia del Bigallo — Before entering the Cathedral, let us take a look at the Loggia del Bigallo (at the corner of Via dei Calzaiuoli, facing the south entrance to the Baptistry). An outstanding example of Florentine Gothic architecture, the Loggia has been attributed to Alberto Arnoldi, head of the *Opera del Duomo* (Cathedral Committee) and dated 1352-1358. It was originally the *Misericordia* (a charitable institution) headquarters until it was turned over to another association, the Bigallo, which put abandoned or orphaned children "on display" so that citizens would take pity on them. Three tabernacles with statues from the school of Nino Pisano (1365) decorate the façade. The lunette below contains a bas-relief of a *Virgin and Child* by Alberto Arnoldi (1361). The loggia has a double arch above which is a row of two-part windows. Inside the building is a 14th century fresco of the *Virgin of Mercy*, especially interesting because it contains a view of Florence of the period.

18

THE CATHEDRAL OF SANTA MARIA DEL FIORE — This
enormous structure was begun by Arnolfo di Cambio in 1296.
Arnolfo had been commissioned by the Republic to create a building "of such great magnificence that man's industry and power
could not surpass it in beauty and size."

The building was to rise on the spot where the church of Santa
Reparata, then cathedral of Florence, stood, right in front of the
Baptistry. When Arnolfo died in 1302 work was suspended and
not resumed until 1334 under the supervision of Giotto, who had
already been named head of the belltower project. Upon the death
of Giotto himself in 1337, work was again held up, but during the
period 1357 to 1364, the *Opera del Duomo* (Cathedral Committee)
decided to expand Arnolfo's original design and turned the project
over to Lapo Ghini and Francesco Talenti.

Finally, in 1366, a definitive plan presented by a team of four
architects was approved and work went on at a steadier pace.
By 1378 the nave roofing was up and between 1380 and 1421

the gallery and the dome drum were completed. In the meantime a competition for the construction of the dome called in 1418 had been won by Filippo Brunelleschi. In fourteen years (1420-1434) Brunelleschi erected the dome which, ever since, has been acclaimed as one of the great architectural wonders of the world. In 1436 Pope Eugene IV solemnly consecrated the church, dedicating it to *Santa Maria del Fiore* (St. Mary of the Flower). Lastly, in 1461, the lantern was put up, a fitting crowning touch to Brunelleschi's dome.

THE FAÇADE — A 19th century Florentine architect, Emilio De Fabris, designed the façade trying to recapture the Florentine Gothic style. This applies to the statuary as well, all of which was sculpted by artists who were contemporaries of De Fabris. The project, which De Fabris worked on until 1871, was continued by Luigi Del Moro who completed it in 1887. The façade is divided into three sections, each of which is topped by a rose window. Below the tallest gable ia a bust of *God the Father* by Augusto Passaglia. The fourteen niches just below it contain busts of famous artists. In the thirteen tabernacles above the portals are statues of the *Apostles*, in the middle of which is a *Virgin and Child*, by Tino Sarrocchi. In the four lower tabernacles (from left to right): a statue of *Bishop Valeriani* who blessed the Cathedral's first stone,

Cathedral - Interior; *right:* **the façade.**

Bishop Tinacci who blessed the first pillar, *Pope Eugene IV* who consecrated the church, and *St. Anthony* who blessed the façade. The left portal is by Passaglia (1897). The partitions are sculptured with scenes of the life of the Virgin *(the Presentation of Mary at the Temple,* the *Marriage of the Virgin)* and personifications of *Temperance, Faith, Humility,* and *Prudence.* In the lunette is an allegorical mosaic (based on a cartoon by Nicolò Barabino) of *Charity enthroned.* The middle portal, also by Passaglia (1903), is decorated with the *Conception and the Coronation of the Virgin,* and, in the lunette, *Christ, the Virgin, and the patrons of the city,* another mosaic by Barabino. In the large gable is the *Virgin in Glory* by Passaglia. The scenes depicted along the right portal (by Giuseppe Cassioli 1899), are the *Expulsion,* the *Assumption,* the *Rest on the flight to Egypt,* the *Visitation,* the *Birth of the Virgin,* and the *Annunciation.* Above is a mosaic symbolizing *Faith being worshipped* based upon cartoons by Barabino.

THE EXTERIOR – The marble facing is in three colors: white from Carrara, green from Prato, and red from the Maremma region. Along the right flank is a fine late 14th century portal known as the *"Porta dei Canonici"* (Door of the Canons), designed and decorated by Giovanni d'Ambrogio and Piero di Giovanni Tedesco. At the corresponding point on the left side is the well-known *Porta della Mandorla,* a forerunner, of Renaissance style sculpture. The portal's name *("mandorla"* means "almond") comes from the shape of the gable with Nanni di Banco's relief of the Virgin (1421). Young Donatello contributed the two statues of *Prophets.* The mosaic in the lunette with an Annunciation is by Domenico Ghirlandaio (1491).

Cathedral - Marble choir screen by Baccio Bandinelli; *right:*
the inside of the dome.

THE INTERIOR — The Florentines wanted their cathedral to be without frills, sober and austere, yet huge in size so the people of the city could assemble inside. In the shape of a Latin cross, the church has single aisles separated from the nave by enormous columns supporting great ribbed vaults. The result is a masterpiece of Florentine Gothic architectural design. The church is 520 feet long, 148 feet wide and 299 feet at the crossing. Inner façade — The stained glass windows over the portals were made from designs by Lorenzo Ghiberti. The mosaic in the lunette above the center portal depicting the *Coronation of the Virgin* has been attributed to the 14th century artist Gaddo Gaddi. On either side are frescoes of *Music-making angels* by Santi di Tito (late 16th century). To the right of the door is the *tomb of Antonio d'Orso, Bishop of Florence* (d. 1321), by the Sienese sculptor, Tino di Camaino (14th century). Above is a clock with four heads of prophets painted on the dial by Paolo Uccello (1443). Right aisle — In the first bay is a medallion with *a bust of Brunelleschi* sculpted by a pupil of the great artist, Andrea Cavalcanti, known as Buggiano (1447). Farther on is a tabernacle, actually wood but made to resemble marble, with a *statue of Isaiah* attributed to Nanni di Banco (1408). The medallion just beyond has a *bust of Giotto* by Benedetto da Maiano (1490). The inscription is by the famous scholar Poliziano. The holy water font with an angel (1380) by the first column is a copy (except for the base) of a fine Gothic original preserved in the Cathedral Museum. In the third bay are two false tomb monuments painted by Bicci di Lorenzo in the 15th century.

24

Cathedral - Santa Reparata, tomb slabs; *right:* **Michelangelo's "Pietà".**

A bust of Marsilio Ficino by Andrea Ferrucci (1521) decorates the medallion of the fourth bay. We enter the huge octagonal choir wholly dominated by Brunelleschi's extraordinary dome. The impressive structure rises 296 feet above ground level (without its lantern which adds another 75 feet) and measures 149 feet across. The inside of the dome is covered with an enormous *Last Judgment* scene frescoed by Giorgio Vasari and Federico Zuccari (1572-1579). The circular stained glass windows around the eight-sided drum were made from designs by Ghiberti, Donatello, Paolo Uccello, and Andrea del Castagno. In the niches of the columns sustaining the dome are eight statues of Apostles, two of which are especially noteworthy (Benedetto da Rovezzano's *St. John*, last column on the right, and Jacopo Sansovino's *St. James the Greater,* left column on the nave side).

In the middle is a carved marble choir rail designed by Giuliano di Baccio d'Agnolo, but sculpted in 1555 by Baccio Bandinelli who, together with Giovanni Bandini, is also responsible for the bas-reliefs around the choir. The *crucifix* on the main altar is by Benedetto da Maiano (1497). Radiating from the choir is the apse in the middle and a transept on either side, all of which are divided into five small chapels. Between the right transept and the apse is the entrance to the **Old Sacristy** with a glazed terracotta *Ascension* scene by Luca della Robbia (1450) overhead. Standing in the main apse chapel is a bronze urn containing relics of *St. Zenobius,* an outstanding example of Lorenzo Ghiberti's great artistry (1432-1442). The bas-reliefs on the front represent scenes from the life of the saint. Between the apse and the left transept is the so-called **New Sacristy** or, more properly, *"Cappella delle Messe"* (Mass Chapel). Here on April 26, 1478 Lorenzo the Magnificent took refuge during the attempt on his life known in history as the Pazzi Conspiracy (his brother Giuliano, not so fortunate, failed to reach safety and was murdered). The terracotta *Resurrection* above the door, dated 1449, was Luca della Robbia's first experiment in ceramic sculpture. The bronze door is a joint effort by della Robbia, Michelozzo, and Maso di Bartolomeo. Inside is a fine basin by Buggiano (1440) with an angel's head attributed to Mino da Fiesole. The inlaid cupboards are by Giuliano da Maiano (1465). Michelangelo's superb *Pietà* of 1550 is in the first chapel of the lefthand transept. Undoubtedly the cathedral's major sculpture, the *Pietà* was never finished by the master who was preparing it for his own tomb. Left aisle: at the fourth bay hangs a well-known painting by Michelino (1465) showing *Dante holding his Divine Comedy.* You see Florence on the left, hell on the right, purgatory in the background, and paradise above. Continuing to the third bay we find Paolo Uccello's famous fresco (transferred on to

Cathedral Museum - Luca della Robbia's choir gallery (detail).

cloth) of the English soldier of fortune, Sir John Hawkwood (1436) and, a bit farther on, Andrea del Castagno's equally famous *Captain Niccolò da Tolentino* (also transferred on to cloth) painted just twenty years later. There is also a noteworthy *bust of Antonio Squarcialupi,* the organist, by Benedetto da Maiano (1490). The statue of the *Prophet Joshua* in the wooden tabernacle of the first bay supposedly represents Poggio Bracciolini, the famous humanist. It has been attributed to Ciuffagni, Nanni di Bartolo, and Donatello. Off the nave is a staircase leading to the crypt of the church of **Santa Reparata,** which originally stood on the site of the present-day cathedral. These fascinating relics of the past (14th century frescos, tomb stones, and architectural elements) came to light after the 1966 flood and were painstakingly restored piece by piece. You can also see the spot where Filippo Brunelleschi, the great architect who designed the cathedral's dome, is buried. At the end of the right aisle is the entrance to the 463-step staircase leading to the dome.

THE CATHEDRAL MUSEUM — In the museum is a fascinating collection of Romanesque architectural remains, statues, and decorative pieces, all of which were originally part of the Cathedral, Baptistry, or once stood in the niches of Giotto's Belltower.

A bust of Brunelleschi, two della Robbia terracottas, and marble bas-reliefs by Baccio Bandinelli are displayed in the vestibule. In the first room to our right we find fragments of the baptismal font which originally stood in the Baptistry. From here we enter the second room which contains the 15th century statues that once decorated the façade of the Cathedral. Donatello's *St. John,* Nanni di Banco's *St. Luke,* and Bernardo Ciuffagni's *St. Matthew* are outstanding. At the far end of the room is a seated statue of *Pope Boniface VIII,* a 14th century piece from the workshop of the Cathedral's first architect, Arnolfo di Cambio, whereas the *Virgin and Child* nearby was carved by the master himself. The drawings of how Arnolfo's original façade looked (before it was demolished in 1588) are especially interesting. The next room contains illuminated manuscripts, reliquaries, enamels, as well as other valuable pieces from the Cathedral treasury. The painting on the altar at the far end is Bernardo Daddi's *Virgin and Child surrounded by saints* (1334). From the second room we enter two newly-opened rooms devoted to Brunelleschi containing a wooden model of his dome and various technical instruments used in erecting it. Retracing our steps through Room 2 we come to the staircase leading to the upper level. On the landing is Donatello's renowned statue of *Mary Magdalen,* originally in the Baptistry, and restored after the 1966 flood.

Cathedral Museum - Donatello's choir gallery (detail).

On the door leading into the main room are two frescoes of heads of Apostles by Bicci di Lorenzo. This room is called the *Sala delle Cantorie* (Choir Gallery Room) after the two carved choir galleries displayed here.

Originally placed over the sacristy doors (old and new) in the Cathedral, the galleries were taken down in 1688. The one near the entrance, by Luca della Robbia (1431-1438), is composed of ten relief panels separated by a row of squared double pilasters. The scene of youths singing and playing instruments so gracefully represented here is an illustration of David's psalm *"Laudate Dominum in sanctis eius."* Opposite is Donatello's choir stall (1433-1438). Here winged cupids joyously dance and cavort behind a row of columns suggesting a loggia. In the same room too are the extraordinary statues Donatello carved for the niches in the Belltower: *Jeremiah, Moses,* and *Habakkuk.* The latter is known as *"lo zuccone"* (the pumpkin-head), due to his baldness. To the right of the entrance is the *Sacrifice of Isaac,* also by Donatello and Nanni di Bartolo. The statues of Sibyls and prophets are by Andrea Pisano. The next room, entered from the right, contains paintings, sculptures, and embroidery. Among the highlights are a *Martyrdom of St. Sebastian,* a 14th century *triptych* by Giovanni del Biondo; a wood inlay with *St. Zenobius and saints* by Giuliano da Maiano; and *Woman with horn of plenty* by Tino di Camaino. Displayed along the walls are several fine 15th century hangings embroidered with scenes from the life of *St. John the Baptist.* They are based upon designs by Antonio del Pollaiolo. At the far end of the room is a magnificent embossed silver and enamel altar. The most renowned Florentine goldsmiths had a hand in the work during the 114 year period (14th-16th century) needed to complete it: Andrea del Verrocchio sculpted the Beheading of St. John, Antonio del Pollaiolo the Birth of St. John, Bernardo Cennini the Visitation to St. Elizabeth, to mention some. The statue of the Baptist in the middle of the front panel is by Michelozzo, while the cross is by Betto Betti, Milano Dei, and Pollaiolo. We cross the room with the choir stalls to enter the room containing the original *reliefs of the Labors of Man, the Liberal Arts, the Holy Sacraments, and the planets,* removed from the Belltower. These panels are by Andrea Pisano and his workshop.

We turn right as we leave the museum and continue back to the Cathedral façade. At the corner we turn right into Via Martelli.

Via de' Martelli — Lined with fine shops and important book stores, this is one of Florence's busiest thoroughfares. A short way up, on the lefthand side, we come to **Palazzo Martelli** and a bit farther on, the **church of San Giovannino.** Across the street on the same side (where the street name changes to Via Cavour) is the renowned Medici-Riccardi Palace.

Palazzo Medici-Riccardi.

THE MEDICI-RICCARDI PALACE — This outstanding building in pure Renaissance style is the masterpiece of Brunelleschi's pupil, Michelozzo Michelozzi. Commissioned by Cosimo the Elder and constructed between 1444 and 1460, it served as Lorenzo the Magnificent's palace. The three storey building has a distinctive rusticated stone exterior rhythmically interspersed with two-part windows and set off by a richly carved cornice. The ground floor windows are a 16th century addition — the corner ones were actually designed by Michelangelo himself. Then, in 1659, the palace was bought by the Riccardi family. They enlarged it on the Via Ginori side by adding seven more to the original core of ten windows. In 1814 the palace came into possession of the Tuscan government and not long afterwards it was turned over to the state. Today the building is the Prefecture headquarters.

An imposing portal leads us into the lovely courtyard with a fine columned patio on the ground floor and an open gallery of Ionic columns on the third floor. Between the arches and the second storey windows are sculpted medallions attributed

Palazzo Medici-Riccardi - Cavalcade fresco by Benozzo
Gozzoli (detail).

to Bertoldo. The graffiti decoration is by Maso di Bartolomeo (1425). On the left of
the entranceway is the **MEDICI MUSEUM** which contains mementos, art works,
documents, and the like, all of which related to the history of the great Florentine
family. Of outstanding interest we might mention a Filippo Lippi *Virgin and Child*
(mid 15th century) and a set of Medici portraits by Bronzino, one of the best-known
16th century Mannerist artists, who was also the Medicis' court painter.
Returning to the courtyard, we take the stairs to the right of the main entrance up
to the palace's remarkable chapel. The entire room including ceiling, stalls, and flooring
was designed by Michelozzo, but its most extraordinary feature is the fresco cycle
which Benozzo Gozzoli painted in 1459-1460 in his lively, colorful narrative style.
In the large fresco ostensibly representing the *Magi on their way to Bethlehem,* Gozzoli
has left us portraits of famous people of the day — primarily members of the Medici
family, as in the case of the youngest Wise Man, actually a portrait of adolescent
Lorenzo the Magnificent. The painting of the *Virgin worshipping the Babe* on the
altar is a 15th century free copy (by Neri di Bicci) of an original by Filippo Lippi.
Returning to the courtyard once more, we take the other staircase up to the *Baroque
gallery* which was built between 1670 and 1688. The ceiling fresco depicting the
Apotheosis of the Medici Family is a fine decorative work by Luca Giordano (1683).

Leaving the palace, we turn right and then take the first street on the right (Via de'
Gori) which leads us into Piazza San Lorenzo.

Church of San Lorenzo - In the photo you can see a bit of the picturesque marketplace which overflows from the square into the surrounding streets.

Piazza San Lorenzo — This picturesque square, also a busy marketplace, is wholly dominated by the simple but imposing *church of San Lorenzo*, and the dome rising above the Princes' Chapel at its far side. To the right of the façade is a *seated statue of Giovanni delle Bande Nere* by Baccio Bandinelli, who also carved the fine reliefs around the square base (1540).

THE CHURCH OF SAN LORENZO — Its origins extend back to the church consecrated in 393 by St. Ambrose, Bishop of Milan, that once stood here. The Romanesque church erected around the year 1000 which replaced it was remodeled between 1421 and 1446 by Brunelleschi who had received the commission from Giovanni Bicci de' Medici, although the project was not finished until 1460 by Brunelleschi's pupil, Antonio Manetti. Michelangelo too, commissioned by his Medici patrons, worked on the great church. He designed the façade on the inside, the Library, and left a design for the outer façade which, however, was never carried out.

THE INTERIOR — The double row of slender Corinthian columns surmounted by rounded arches rhythmically spaced along the nave and the typically Brunelleschian grey *(pietra serena)* and white (plaster) color scheme combine to create an effect of incomparable harmony and elegance. The balcony high up on the inner façade was

32

designed by Michelangelo. The two facing pulpits at the last bays along the nave are the last works of Donatello, who was working on them when he died in 1466. They were finished by his pupils, Bertoldo and Bellano. The panels of the *Crucifixion* and *Deposition from the Cross* (on the left pulpit), intensely dramatic renderings of these familiar subjects, are especially outstanding. Along the right aisle (second chapel) is Rosso Fiorentino's *Marriage of the Virgin,* a fine 16th century painting, and further on (last bay) is Desiderio da Settignano's carved marble *tabernacle,* a masterpiece of 15th century sculpture. Along the left aisle (last bay) is a fresco by Bronzino, the *Martyrdom of St. Lawrence* (1569). At the foot of the little stairway before the main altar, a bronze grating marks the spot where Cosimo the Elder, called *"Pater Patriae"* (father of his country) is buried. From the far side of the left transept we enter the **Sacrestia Vecchia,** or Old Sacristy. Despite its small size, it ranks as one of Brunelleschi's finest creations, an outstanding example of spatial harmony achieved by combining rhythmic and geometric effects. The painted stucco medallions in the pendentives of the hemispherical dome which illustrate *scenes from the life of John the Baptist* are by Donatello, as are the four *Evangelists* in the lunettes, the *frieze with cherubs,* the two bronze portals on either side of the altar with *Fathers of the Church* and *Apostles* on the panels, and the magnificent terracotta bust of *St. Lawrence* on the cabinet. The sarcophagi in the middle, sculpted by Andrea Cavalcanti, *"il Buggiano,"* are the tombs of Giovanni Bicci and Piccarda de' Medici, Cosimo the Elder's parents, while the bronze and prophyry one on the left beneath the archway, a masterpiece by Verrocchio (1472), is the burial place of Cosimo's sons, Giovanni and Piero. Returning to the church proper, we enter (on the right) the 14th century **Martelli Chapel** with a lovely 15th century Filippo Lippi *Annunciation* on the altar and a *tomb monument to Donatello* on the righthand wall which was sculpted in 1896 by Romanelli. From here you may go directly into the main cloister and the Laurentian Library.

33

San Lorenzo Church - Interior.

The Laurentian Library — The library, reached from the square at number 9 (alongside the church) is at the far end of a lovely, 15th century Brunelleschian-style cloister, up a flight of stairs. Founded by Cosimo the Elder and later enlarged by Lorenzo the Magnificent, this is one of the world's finest libraries. It was wholly designed by Michelangelo, although the vestibule which Michelangelo started work on in 1524 was completed by Vasari and other architects. Its incomparable collections include codices, manuscripts, and illuminated missals dating from the 6th to 15th centuries, Lorenzo the Magnificent's prayerbook, and autographs of famous personages ranging from Petrarch to Napoleon. The reading room, nearly 165 feet long, is lit by 15 stained glass windows designed by Giovanni da Udine. The wooden ceiling, desks, and lecterns were all designed by Michelangelo.

Once more back in Piazza San Lorenzo, we continue along the right side of the church building and turn left at the corner, until reaching Piazza degli Aldobrandini (behind the church) where we enter the Medici Chapels.

The Medici Chapels.

THE MEDICI CHAPELS – Building on this incredible structure was started in 1604 by Matteo Nigetti. The plans were drawn up by Prince Giovanni de' Medici, halfbrother of Grandduke Cosimo I, whose idea it was to erect a family burial chamber worthy of the Medici's power and wealth. It thus became fittingly known as the Chapel of the Princes.

From the vast low ceilinged crypt we go up the stairs to the **Chapel of the Princes,** a huge Baroque hall lined from floor to ceiling with multicolored marbles, precious stones, and gilded bronze. The dome frescoes with *scenes from the Old and New Testaments* were painted by Pietro Benvenuti in 1829. The striking coats-of-arms, sixteen in all, along the lower register of wall decoration are actually mosaics made out of precious stones. They represent the Tuscan cities which were part of the Medici grandduchy. Above the bronze sarcophagi — the tombs of the Medici granddukes

Medici Chapels - Chapel of the Princes entirely lined with precious marbles and gemstones. It was begun early in the 16th century by Nigetti, but its construction went on till the end of the 17th century.

Medici Chapels - Supper at Emmaus, detail of the main altar of the Chapel of the Princes.

**Medici Chapels - The tomb of Lorenzo, Duke of Urbino,
by Michelangelo.**

from Cosimo I (not to be confused with Cosimo the Elder) to Cosimo III — stand impressive bronze statues by Pietro Tacca (17th century). Behind the elaborate altar inlaid with precious stones are two little rooms with a collection of priceless gold and silver reliquaries displayed in showcases.

Returning to the entrance we follow the lefthand corridor to the **New Sacristy** — called "new" to distinguish it from the earlier Old Sacristy inside the church.

Although both sacristies have the same square-shaped plan, the *Sacrestia Nuova* is considerably more somber-looking, as befits a sepulchral chamber. Designed and built by Michelangelo between 1520 and 1533, it was left unfinished until Vasari completed it in 1557. Michelangelo conceived the architecture and sculpture as a part of a single decorative scheme, although only two of the three tombs planned

Medici Chapels - The tomb of Giuliano, Duke of Nemours, by Michelangelo.

for the chamber were ever finished. To the left of the entrance is the *tomb of Lorenzo, Duke of Urbino* (Lorenzo the Magnificent's nephew), depicted engrossed in thought. Figures representing *Dusk* and *Dawn* decorate the sarcophagus lid. Opposite is the *tomb of Giuliano, Duke of Nemours* (Lorenzo the Magnificent's son). A symbol of action, he is dressed in a suit of armor and holds a baton which stands for command. The figures at his feet represent *Day* and *Night*. The third tomb, never finished, was intended for both Lorenzo the Magnificent and his brother, Giuliano (although only Giuliano, murdered in the Pazzi Conspiracy of 1472, is buried here). Michelangelo himself carved the group of the *Virgin with the Babe at her breast,* endowing the youthful figure of Mary with dignified nobility. The figures of Sts. Cosmas and Damian on either side are by pupils of the master, Montorsoli and Raffaello da Montelupo.

SECOND ITINERARY

Piazza del Duomo - Via Calzaiuoli - Church of Orsanmichele - Piazza della Signoria (Loggia della Signoria, Palazzo Vecchio) - Piazzale degli Uffizi (Uffizi Gallery).

Via de' Calzaiuoli — This shop- and boutique-lined thoroughfare connects Piazza della Signoria and Piazza del Duomo. Just off Piazza del Duomo, plaques on buildings indicate the sites of the studios where Donatello and Michelozzo worked.
Further on, a few yards beyond Via Tosinghi, Via del Corso (a street once famous as the scene of a periodic horse race) intersects Via dei Calzaiuoli and continues as Via degli Speziali on the right. If you turn into Via degli Speziali, you soon come to a bustling square, dating from the 19th century, Piazza della Repubblica. If, instead you go staight on towards Piazza della Signoria, you will note, on the right side, a Gothic building that looks like some kind of protective tower, although it is actually the church of Orsanmichele.

THE CHURCH OF ORSANMICHELE — When Arnolfo di Cambio built it in 1290 he had to tear down the church of San Michele Arcangelo then on the site. Since San Michele was located by a truck garden (*orto* in Italian) it came to be known as Orsanmichele. Arnolfo's open arcade was the "*loggia del grano*" (wheat arcade), the place where wheat dealers carried on their bargaining. When it was destroyed in a fire in the 14th century, it was rebuilt by the foremost Florentine architects of the day, namely Francesco Talenti, Neri di Fioravante, Benci di Cione, and Simone di Francesco Talenti. Their design included an upper storey above the loggia which would serve as a granary for storing wheat that could feed the citizens during emergencies such as sieges. The building, commissioned by the Republic of Florence itself, was begun in 1337 and fully completed in 1404. In 1349, during construction, it was decided that the open loggia should be turned into an oratory, although not until 1380 did Simone di Francesco Talenti receive the commission to wall in the open arches. He brilliantly solved the problem by putting in superb portals so delicately patterned that they convey the effect of stone lace.

The statues decorating the niches on all four sides of the building represent the patron saints of the *Arti Maggiori* (Guilds).
Commissioned from the great sculptors of the 14th, 15th, and 16th centuries such as Nanni di Banco, Donatello, Giambologna, and others, the statues represent a veritable history of the development of Florentine Renaissance sculpture.

Starting from the left of the entrance on Via de' Calzaiuoli: the Wool Guild tabernacle with *St. John the Baptist* by Lorenzo Ghiberti (1414-1416); 2) the Court of Commerce tabernacle by Donatello and Michelozzo with bronze statues of *Christ and St. Thomas* by Verrocchio (1464-1483) and 3) the Judges' and Notaries' Guild tabernacle with *St. Luke* by Giambologna (1601). Along Via Orsanmichele side: the Butchers' Guild tabernacle with *St. Peter* by Donatello (1408); 2) the Shoemakers' Guild tabernacle with *St. Philip* by Nanni di Banco (1405-1410); 3) the Builders' and Sculptors' Guild tabernacle with "*Quattro Coronati*" (four saints) by Nanni di Banco (1408); 4) the Gunsmiths' tabernacle with a copy of Donatello's *St. George* (the original, dated 1416, has been moved to the Bargello Museum). The extraordinary relief carving of *St. George killing the Dragon* beneath the statue is also by Donatello.

Orsanmichele - Entrance.

Along Via della Lana: 1) the Moneychangers' Guild tabernacle with *St. Lawrence* by Lorenzo Ghiberti (1420), the Wool Guild tabernacle with *St. Stephen* by Lorenzo Ghiberti (1428); 3) the Blacksmiths' Guild tabernacle with *St. Eligius* by Nanni di Banco (1415). Between the St. Lawrence and St. Stephan niches is the main church entrance with carved decoration by Nicola Lamberti.

Along Via dei Lamberti: 1) the Flaxmakers' Guild tabernacle with *St. Mark* by Donatello (1411-1413); 2) the Furriers' Guild tabernacle with a *St. Jacob* and a bas-relief attributed to Ciuffagni; 3) the Physicians' and Pharmacists' Guild tabernacle with a *Virgin and Child* (known as the "Virgin of the Rose") attributed to Simone Talenti; 4) the Silkmakers' Guild tabernacle with *St. John the Evangelist* by Baccio da Montelupo (1515). The glazed terracotta medallions are by Luca della Robbia except for the one over the tabernacle of the Butchers' Guild which is modern (it comes from the renowned Ginori ceramic factory).

You may enter the church from either the main entrance on Via Arte della Lana or the secondary one on Via dei Calzaiuoli.

THE INTERIOR — The simple rectangular space, divided into two parts, is illuminated by glowing stained glass windows. The ceiling is covered with 14th and 15th century frescoes of the guilds' patron saints. Dominating the interior is Orcagna's huge canopied **tabernacle** of 1349-1359, an impressive masterpiece of the International Gothic style (the influence of this style was being felt in Florence towards the mid 1300s). The relief panels around the base depict scenes from the life of the Virgin. Starting from the *Birth of the Virgin*, the story continues with the *Presentation of Mary at the Temple*, the *Marriage of the Virgin*, the *Annunciation*, the *Nativity*, the *Presentation*

41

Palazzo dell'Arte della Lana - *Left:* **Orsanmichele - Orcagna's tabernacle.**

of Jesus at the Temple, the *Annunciation of the Death of the Virgin.* The statues on the columns represent *Prophets, Sibyls, Virtues,* and *Apostles* with a figure of the *Savior* on the top of the dome. Of all the reliefs, the finest is the *Assumption of the Virgin* on the back. The clean-shaven man wrapped in a hood is a self-portrait of the artist. The panel of the *Madonna delle Grazie* on the altar, dated 1352, is by Bernardo Orcagna. On the altar to the left of the tabernacle is a marble group, the *Virgin and S. Anne,* by Francesco da Sangallo (1526).

Leaving the church from the main door, we are in front of the **Palazzo dell'Arte della Lana** (the Woolmakers' Guild) which is joined to the church by a raised passageway. Built in 1300, it was the headquarters of one of Florence's wealthiest guilds. Then, in 1905, it was restored and turned over to the local Dante Society. Inside, traces of 15th century frescoes are still visible. On the corner of the building is a lovely Gothic tabernacle known as "St. Mary of the Trumpet", containing a 14th century painting of the *Virgin with Angels* and *Saints* and the *Coronation of the Virgin* by Jacopo Landini known as *"il Casentino."* Originally displayed in the nearby Piazza del Mercato Vecchio, it was moved to its present location when the area around the square, the old city center, was torn down in the 19th century.

Back on Via dei Calzaiuoli there is a charming little church opposite Orsanmichele, **San Carlo dei Lombardi.** Begun in 1349 by Neri Fioravanti and Benci di Cione, it was finished by Simone Talenti in 1384. Inside is a 14th century painting by Niccolò Gerini, a dramatic rendering of the *Burial of Christ.*

43

Piazza della Signoria - The square is dominated by the towering structure of Palazzo Vecchio. On the right is the Loggia della Signoria. The square has been the center of city life for centuries.

PIAZZA DELLA SIGNORIA — This square of insuperable beauty and dignity is full of exciting monuments: Palazzo Vecchio, the Loggia della Signoria, old palaces, the fountain — not to mention a host of important statues. The effect is an unforgettable vision of grandeur and power. In fact, over the centuries, the square has been witness to the great historical and political events in Florence, all of which have taken place here. Here Florence fought her bitter internal struggles, here she affirmed her power and glory, and from here Florentine civilization was propagated throughout the whole world.

Before entering Palazzo Vecchio, we shall stop to look at the fascinating objects surrounding us in the square. To the left of the palace is Bartolomeo Ammannati's imposing **Neptune Fountain** (1563-1575). The Florentines, never particularly fond of the huge Neptune in the middle, immediately dubbed it *"il Biancone"* (the big

white lump) and made up a little rhyme about it to express their disdain: "*Ammannato, Ammannato, che bel marmo hai rovinato*" (Ammannato, Ammannato what nice marble you had to garble). In contrast, the *bronze sea nymphs and satyrs* around the fountain, by Ammannati and Giambologna (and others), received high praise from all. A few yards away from the fountain towards the center of the square you will see a porphyry disk in the pavement. The inscription recalls that on this spot on May 23, 1498 the fiery reformer monk Girolamo Savonarola and his followers, Fra Domenico Buonvicini da Pisa and Fra Silvestro Maruffi, were hanged and burned at the stake as heretics. Opposite the fountain is an imposing *equestrian monument to Cosimo I de´ Medici* by Giambologna (1594). The reliefs around the base represent: *The Tuscan Senate confering the title of grandduke on Cosimo I* (1537), *Pius V presenting Cosimo with the insignia of the rank of grandduke* (1569), and *Cosimo victoriously entering Siena* (1557). Beyond the statue where the square fans out in back are two extraordinary old buildings: the 14th century **Palazzo del Tribunale di Mercanzia** (no. 10) and the 16th century **Palazzo Uguccioni** (no. 7) designed by Mariotto di Zanobi. The building directly opposite Palazzo Vecchio, the headquarters of an insurance company, was designed in 1871 by Landi who tried to recreate the Florentine medieval style.

Equestrian monument to Grandduke Cosimo I de' Medici by
Giambologna; *right:* Ammannati's Fountain.

The Loggia della Signoria - *Right:* Rape of the Sabine Women
by Giambologna.

THE LOGGIA DELLA SIGNORIA — To the right of Palazzo Vecchio
is the elegant open arcade known as the Loggia della Signoria.
Considered a masterpiece of late Gothic architecture, it nevertheless
foreshadows the Renaissance style on the horizon. The loggia is
also known by two other names, the Loggia dei Lanzi since, in the
16th century, palace guards in the service of Cosimo I called
Lanzichenecchi were stationed here, and the Loggia dell'Orcagna
because of the traditional (erroneous) attribution of the design to
the 14th century artist, Orcagna. Responsible for the project instead
were the architects who also worked on the Cathedral, namely
Benci di Cioni, Simone Talenti, and others. It was put up between
1376 and 1381.

The Loggia della Signoria - Interior; *right:* **Perseus by Cellini.**

On either side of the staircase leading up to the arcade is a stone lion. However, the one on the right is an authentic Classical sculpture, whereas the one on the left is a 17th century copy carved by a Roman sculptor, Flamino Vacca. The statues under the loggia are a mixture of antique Roman and 16th century Florentine works. Beneath the left arch is one of the great masterpieces of Renaissance art, Benvenuto Cellini's bronze *Perseus* (1533). Perseus is portrayed triumphantly holding aloft the severed head of the monstruous Medusa whom he has just slain. The bronze relief panel on the base (a copy of the original now in the Bargello Museum) shows *Perseus freeing Andromeda*. The four bronze statuettes around the base represent Mercury, Minerva, Jupiter, and Danae (the latter were Perseus' parents). Beneath the righthand arch is another famous work, Giambologna's marble masterpiece of the *Rape of the Sabine women* (1583). The relief on the pedestal, by the same artist, shows the Romans carrying off the Sabines. Behind the Rape of the Sabine women is another statue by Giambologna, *Hercules and the centaur Nessus* (1599). In the center is *Menelaus carrying the body of Patrocles,* a restored copy of a 4th century B.C. Greek original. Behind the Perseus is the *Rape of Polyxena,* by Pio Fedi (1866). The statues against the wall, Roman works dating from the Imperial period, represent matrons, vestal virgins, and priestesses, with the exception of the third from the left (the sorrowing figure has been identified as Tusnelda, a symbol of vanquished Germany).

The flag-throwers of the costume football game - *Right:*
Palazzo Vecchio.

PALAZZO VECCHIO (OR PALAZZO DELLA SIGNORIA) — This
building ranks as one of Florence's most important architectural
monuments and indeed as one of the major medieval civic buildings
of the Italian peninsula. It rises impressive and austere to dominate
Piazza Signoria, its over 300-foot tower soaring asymmetrically
from the façade to add a touch of elegance to the overall severe
appearance. Although traditionally ascribed to Arnolfo di Cambio
(who supposedly modelled it on the Castle of Poppi belonging to
the counts Guidi and put it up between 1298 and 1314), this attribution has never been corroborated by any documentary evidence.
The original construction, rectangular in shape, has a distinctive
rusticated stone facing pierced by a double row of two-part Gothic
windows topped by crenellation. The off center position of the
rectangular tower (known as Arnolfo's Tower) is due to the fact
that it was built over a pre-existing one, the Foraboschi Tower.
The symbols of Florence, a fleur-de-lis and a lion, proudly crown
the whole. Numerous additions were put on the building: in 1343

**Piazza della Signoria - Copy of Michelangelo's David
(the original is in the Academy Gallery).**

on the Via della Ninna (south) side, between 1495 to 1511 on the Via dei Gondi (north), side, and lastly, in 1593 on the Via dei Leoni (east) side. The last addition, commissioned by Cosimo I and started by Buontalenti, was designed by Vasari, whose work was nevertheless in keeping with the original style.

Shields with the emblems of the cities making up the Republic of Florence lend a note of color in the space below the protruding upper floor. Over the entrance are two lions (1528). The inscription over the monogram of Christ reads "*Rex Regum et Dominus Dominantium*" (King of Kings and lord of lords). Put up in 1551, it commemorates the last years of the Republic when the Florentines elected Christ as their king (1529). The palace, the seat of the city's governing body (the *Signoria*), was the residence of the Duke of Athens (1342-1343) and two centuries later (1540-1550) of Cosimo I who left it in 1550 when he moved into Palazzo Pitti. In 1848-1849 and 1859-1860, during the struggle for the unification of Italy, it served as headquarters for various provisional governments. Then, from 1865 to 1871, when Florence

Piazza della Signoria - Hercules and Cacus by Baccio Bandinelli.

was for a short time capital of the newly-united kingdom of Italy, Palazzo Vecchio was the Chamber of Deputies of the Italian state. Since 1872 it has been Florence's town hall. The broad landing extending before Palazzo Vecchio is called *"l'arringhiera"* (the haranging place), because from up here public speakers addressed the crowds. It is a veritable showcase of masterpieces of sculpture. From left to right: Donatello's *"Marzocco" lion,* symbol of the Republic of Florence, holding a shield with the Florentine fleur-de-lis on it (this is a copy of the original dated 1438, now in the Bargello National Museum). Next, on a column pedestal, is an original bronze by Donatello of 1460. A representation of the biblical *Judith* slaying the tyrant Holofernes, it was supposed to remind the Florentines of the time the Duke of Athens was driven out of the city and, as such, has always stood for the Florentine's love of liberty.

By the entrance is a 19th century copy of Michelangelo's *David* (the original stood here from 1503 to 1873 when it was moved to the Academy Gallery for safekeeping). Lastly, *Hercules and Cacus* by Baccio Bandinelli (1533) pales in such illustrious company. The pair of *Hermes figures* (half-man, half-tree) by the door (the one on the left by Vincenzo de' Rossi and the one on the right by Giambologna) originally supported the chain which closed off the entranceway.

Palazzo Vecchio - Michelozzo's courtyard dated 1453. In the middle is Tadda's 16th century porphyry fountain surmounted by a copy of Verrocchio's Cupid with a Dolphin. *Above:* Verrocchio's original, displayed in the Sala della Cancelleria.

THE INTERIOR – The **courtyard** is a charming introduction to the palace. The harmonious Renaissance-style arcade was designed by Michelozzo in 1453, although the frescoes and stucco decoration on the columns (recently restored to their original splendor) were not added until 1565.

The courtyard was decorated in honor of Joan of Austria when she wed Francesco de' Medici (in fact, the frescoes represent the possessions of the Austrian crown). In the center of the courtyard is a *porphyry fountain* designed by Vasari and crafted by Battista del Tadda 1557. It is decorated with a charming winged cupid holding a fish, actually a copy of Verrocchio's original of 1476 recently moved upstairs (3rd floor, *Sala della Cancelleria*) for safekeeping. In a niche under the portico is a marble group of *Samson and the Philistine* by Pierino da Vinci. At the far left end is the entrance to the **Sala delle Armi** (Weapons Room), which, unlike most of the palace, retains its original 14th century appearance. Continuing to the second courtyard, we note the sturdy columns that Cronaca designed to support the incredible weight of the Hall of the 500 directly overhead. To reach the Hall of the 500 we may take either of the staircases (designed by Vasari) located between the two courtyards.

THE SECOND FLOOR – **The Hall of the 500** is of truly grandiose proportions: 173 feet long, 71 feet wide, and 58 feet high. Built by Simone del Pollaiolo in 1495 after the Medicis had been driven out of the city (in 1494) and a republic with Savonarola at its head replaced them, it was used for meetings of the People's Great Assembly, composed of 500 citizens. When the Medicis were reinstated in 1512, Cosimo I commissioned Baccio d'Agnolo and Baccio Bandinelli to redo the hall so it could be used for receptions and public audiences, Later, Giorgio Vasari, a writer as well as painter and architect, enlarged it and added the fresco decoration (1560-1572).

Actually, in 1503 Pier Soderini, a leading city official, had commissioned Leonardo da Vinci and Michelangelo to each decorate a wall with frescoes commemorating famous Florentine battles. But nothing ever came of the project, except for a preliminary design for the Battle of Anghiari (Leonardo) and one for an episode of the war against Pisa (Michelangelo), the cartoons of which have either been lost or destroyed. The frescoes we see today, by Vasari, represent the triumphs of Grandduke Cosimo I and episodes of the war waged by the Florentines against the Pisans and the Sienese. From the entrance, upper register: *Cosimo I founds the Order of the Knights of St.*

57

Palazzo Vecchio -
The Hall of the 500,
built by Cronaca
in 1495 and later
remodeled by Vasari.
Left: Victory of
Genius over Brute
Force by
Michelangelo. The
marble group was
carved in 1525 for
the tomb of Julius II
in Rome.

Stephen by Passignano and in the three big panels below: *The Florentines defeat the Pisans at Torre San Vincenzo;* 2) *Emperor Maximilian attempts to capture Leghorn;* 3) *The Florentines attack Pisa.* In the upper righthand corner is *Boniface VIII receiving the ambassadors from Florence* by Ligozzi. Below is a statue of *Cosimo I* by Bandinelli. The subjects of the *tapestries,* below the frescoes, woven in the Medici tapestry works, are scenes from the life of St. John the Baptist. They were inspired by Andrea del Sarto's frescoes of the subject in the *Chiostro dello Scalzo* on nearby Via Cavour. The statues along the walls by Vincenzo de' Rossi represent the *Labors of Hercules.* The elaborate ceiling is divided into 39 compartments. The paintings, by Vasari and his helpers, portray the history of Florence and the Medici family with the *Triumph of Cosimo I* in the center. The door at the far end (generally locked) leads to the **ricetto** (entrance hall) decorated by Lorenzo Sabatini and the **Sala degli Otto di Pratica** with a magnificent carved wood ceiling by Benedetto da Maiano and Marco del Tasso and 18th century Gobelins tapestries decorating the walls. From the *ricetto* we enter the **Sala del Duecento** (Hall of the 200). It was named Hall of the 200 because the Council of 200 (citizens) used to meet here at the time of the Republic to deliberate major decisions. The hall was designed by Benedetto and Giuliano da Maiano (1472-1477). Giuliano also designed the lovely ceiling decorated with carved fleur-de-lis. The superb *tapestries* on the walls, woven in Florence, show scenes from the life of Joseph. These rooms are now used by the mayor and the town council. Returning to the Hall of the 500, we turn to the wall to the left of the entranceway which has three huge arched windows and a platform where the grandduke would sit during public audiences. This zone of the hall was aptly known as l'**Udienza** (the Audience). The statues in the niches are, from left to right, *Giovanni delle Bande Nere* by Bandinelli, *Leo X,* by Bandinelli and Vincenzo de' Rossi, and *Alessandro de' Medici* by Bandinelli. Righthand wall (from left to right): in the niche *Pope Clement VII crowning*

Hall of the 500 - The siege and conquest of Pisa by Vasari (detail);
right: **Francesco I's Study.**

Charles V, marble group by Bandinelli and Giovanni Caccini, to the right, statue of
Francis I by Caccini; above, *Cosimo receiving the insignia from Pius V,* painting on
slate by Cigoli. Next are three huge frescoes by Vasari: 1) *the Capture of Siena;* 2)
the Capture of Porto Ercole and 3) *the Victory of Marciano.* Above right, *Cosimo is
proclaimed Duke by the Florentine Senate* by Cigoli. At the far end of the room in the
large center niche is marble group by Michelangelo dated 1525 representing the *Victory
of Genius over brute force.* Carved for the tomb of Pope Julius in Rome, it was placed
here in 1921 to commemorate the Italian victory at Vittorio Veneto during World War I
(1918). The niches on either side contain antique statues, considerably restored, of
Leda, Mercury, Apollo and *Bacchus.*

To the right, not far from Michelangelo's statue, is the door leading into the so-called
Studiolo of Francesco I. This charming little study was designed by Vasari (1570-
1572) as a place where the scholarly and art loving prince could close himself off
from the world. Every square inch is decorated: there are paintings, frescoes, bronze
statuettes, as well as stucco decoration and inlays. The ceiling panels are by Francesco
Morandini, known as *"il Poppi."* The slate portraits in the lunette by Bronzino are of
Francesco's parents, *Cosimo I and Eleanor of Toledo.* The closet doors are decorated
with mythological scenes and historical episodes painted by two famous 16th century
Florence Mannerists, Bronzino and Allori. In the eight niches along the upper section
of the wall are lovely bronze statuettes representing mythological divinities; Giambologna's *Apollo* (last, right wall) and Ammannati's *Venus* (opposite the Apollo)
are outstanding. From the left side, through a tiny door disguised as a cabinet, we
can enter the **Tesoretto,** the secret writing room that Vasari created for Cosimo I.

By way of the Hall of the 500; we enter the **Quartiere of Leo X** (these apartments
are not always open to the public as they are part of the mayor's offices). Frescoed
with scenes of Medici history by Vasari and his helpers, the rooms are named after
famous Medicis: **Sala di Leone X** (communicating with a tiny chapel which has
an old copy of Raphael's *Madonna dell'Impannata;* **Sala di Clemente VII** (with a
famous fresco of Florence during the siege of 1529); **Sala di Giovanni delle Bande
Nere; Sala di Cosimo il Vecchio, Sala di Lorenzo il Magnifico,** and **Sala di
Cosimo I.**

Palazzo Vecchio - Hall of Leo X.

THE THIRD FLOOR — From the *Sala di Leone X,* we can either take the stairs to the third floor or else return to the Hall of the 500 and take the elevator by Michelangelo's statue of Victory. To the left, off the top landing, is the entrance to the **Quartiere degli Elementi,** a suite designed by Bernardo del Tasso (1550). The name *"degli elementi"* comes from the frescoes by Vasari and Cristoforo Gherardi (known as *"il Doceno"*) with representations of the elements of *fire, water, earth* and *air,* exalting the glory of the Medici. From the *Sala degli Elementi* we enter the **Terrazzo di Saturno** which gets its name from the allegory of *Saturn devouring his children* on the ceiling. The *terrazzo* commands a splendid panoramic view of the city surrounded by the hills of Settignano, Piazzale Michelangelo, and Forte Belvedere. From the left we enter the **Sala di Ercole.** The ceiling fresco by Gherardi represents the *Labors of Hercules.* On the wall is a 16th century Florentine tapestry depicting *Hercules slaying the Centaur* after a drawing by Stradano. From the **Sala di Giove** with a ceiling fresco of the *Childhood of Jupiter,* we come back to the *Sala degli Elementi* and from here, taking the door on the right, we enter the **Camera di Berecinzia,** with Florentine allegorical tapestries and the *Triumph of Berecinzia* and the *Four Seasons* on the ceiling by Vasari and Gherardi. Next is the **Sala di Cerere** with a fresco of *Ceres in search of Proserpine* by Gherardi. The tapestries, after cartoons by Stradano, show hunting scenes. A door at the far end leads to the **Writing Room** (or **Sala di Calliope,** from Vasari's ceiling fresco). Here Cosimo I used to work on his collection of precious *objets d'art* (jewelry, miniatures, and bronzes) now displayed in the Pitti Palace.

Leaving the *Quartiere degli Elementi* on our way to the **Quartiere di Eleonora di Toledo** we cross the Hall of the 500 by way of the overhead passage which commands a superb bird's eye view of the huge hall. The suite was designed for Eleanor, Cosimo I's wife, by Vasari who, in 1562, renovated the apartments which originally served as the priors' residence. The small vestibule decorated with a *Virgin* attributed to Rossello di Iacopo Franchi leads to the **Sala Verde** (Green Room) which gets its name from

Palazzo Vecchio - Chapel of the Priors.

the painted ceiling with the so-called grotesque style decoration by Ridolfo del Ghirlandaio. To the left is the **Studiolo di Eleonora** (Eleanora's Study) with a ceiling fresco by Salviati. To the right is the **Chapel** frescoed by Bronzino in the 1560s and an one of the Mannerist artist's most ambitious undertakings. On the altar is a *Pietà* and an *Annunciation.* Along the walls are three stories from the life of Moses: the *Crossing of the Red Sea,* the *Bronze Serpent,* and *Moses making water flow from a rock.* From the Sala Verde we enter the apartments that Vasari rebuilt for Eleonora. The ceilings were decorated by Bernardo del Tasso. The frescoes of feats performed by famous women (for which each room is named) were painted by Stradano after cartoons created by Vasari himself. The first room we see, the **Camera delle Sabine** (the Sabine Women Room), was assigned to Eleonora's ladies-in-waiting. The ceiling fresco shows the *Sabine women between the Roman and Sabine soldiers.* There are two paintings depicting the *Virgin and Child* on the wall, one by Lorenzo di Credi, the other by Andrea del Sarto. The portraits of young Medici are in the style of Sustermans, the Flemish master who took up residence in Florence. Next we come to the **Stanza di Ester** (Esther Room), or the Dining Room. The ceiling fresco of *Ahasuerus crowning Esther* is by Stradano. In addition there are a splendid carved marble basin and three splendid tapestries of Spring, Fall, and the Sun Chariot. The **Stanza di Penelope** (Penelope's Room) has a fresco of *Penelope at her loom* on the ceiling with other episodes from the Odyssey around the frieze. The room is hung with *tapestries,* one representing Summer and the other Fall. The view of Piazza della Signoria from the windows is superb. Lastly, we come to the **Stanza della Bella Gualdrada** (the Room of the Fair Gualdrada) which was Eleonora's private chamber. On the ceiling is a fresco depicting *Gualdrada refusing to kiss Emperor Otto* while along the frieze are scenes of festivals held in Florence's main squares and streets. From here we enter a narrow passegeway — in which Dante's death mask is displayed — leading to the **Cappella della Signoria** (Chapel). This section of the building and the Hall of the 200 are all that remains of the Priors' Apartments dating from Florence's Republican period. The monk Girolamo Savonarola and his two followers spent the

63

Palazzo Vecchio - Hall of the Lilies.

night before they were burned at the stake praying here. The frescoes are by Ridolfo del Ghirlandaio (1514), whereas the Holy Family on the altar is by Mariotta da Pescia. The following rooms were decorated at the time of the Republic. The **Audience Hall** with fine frescoes by Francesco Salviati (1550-1560) portraying scenes from the life of Camillus was designed by Benedetto da Maiano in the late 1400s.

Particularly noteworthy is the carved marble and porphyry doorway surmounted by a statue of Justice also by a Maiano (1476-1478). The *wood inlay doors* with Dante and Petrarch depicted on them are by Giuliano da Maiano and Francione (1481). On the **Sala dei Gigli** (Lily Room) side of the doorway are statues of *St. John the Baptist* and little cupids, again by Maiano (1476-1478). The incredible carved wooden ceiling is by Giuliano da Maiano. The walls are covered with a gold fleur-de-lis pattern on a blue ground (and thus the name of the room) which stands for the alliance the Florentine Republic accorded with the Royal House of France. Facing the entrance is a huge fresco with illusionistic architecture by Domenico Ghirlandaio and his helpers (1481-1485). From left to right we see: *Brutus, Mutius Scevola, Camillus, St. Zenobius between Sts. Lawrence and Stephen, Decius, Scipio, and Cicero.* The door cut into the wall on the lefthand side leads to the **Chancellory.** The room has been dedicated to the most renowned of the Florentine chancellors, Machiavelli, of whom there are two portraits: a painted plaster bust and a posthumous oil portrait painted in the late

64

Palazzo Vecchio - Map Room.

16th century by Santi di Tito. The *Winged Cupid holding a fish* on a pedestal in the middle of the room is the original Verrocchio (1476), once part of the main courtyard fountain, and moved here for preservation. Back in the *Sala dei Gigli,* the door beneath Ghirlandaio's frescoes, leads to the **Guardaroba Mediceo** or **Map Room** from the 33 maps painted on the cupboard doors by the famous mathematician, Fra Ignazio Danti (1563-1575) and Don Stefano Buonsignori (1575-1584). A door between the cupboards in the righthand corner of the room leads to a terrace from which you can view the oldest section of the building and reach the *"studiolo"* where Cellini used to repair the Medici jewelry. From the iron grate Cosimo I would spy into the great hall below. Leaving the *Sala dei Gigli* from the door on the right, we take the stairway to the passageway that skirts the outer part of the building. From here we get a magnificent panoramic view of the city. Climbing the tower, we reach the tiny cell dubbed *"l'alberghetto"* (the little hotel) where Cosimo the Elder was kept prisoner before being sent off to exile (1433) and which was Savonarola's prison from April 8 to May 23, 1498. From the top of the tower the view of Florence and the surrounding countryside is truly unforgettable. On the way down we stop off at the **Loeser Collection** on the mezzanine. The paintings and sculpture from the 14th to 16th century Tuscan schools were bequeathed to the city of Florence by a well-known American art collector, Charles Loeser, who died in 1928.

The Piazzale of the Uffizi - Splendid construction by Vasari, the arcaded building makes a marvelous frame for Piazza Signoria on one side and the river on the other. Soaring above the arcade is the tower of Palazzo Vecchio.

Piazzale degli Uffizi — The impressive arcade running from the south side of Palazzo Vecchio and ending in an arch, which is like a huge picture frame for the Arno beyond, was designed by Vasari. The imposing three-sided building now housing both the Uffizi Galleri and the State Archives was commissioned by Cosimo I as government offices. Begun in 1560 and considered Vasari's architectural masterpiece, it was actually finished in 1580 by Alfonso Parigi and Bernardo Buontalenti. During the mid 1800s statues of famous Tuscans were sculpted for the niches along the arcade, but aside from the *St. Antonino* by Giovanni Duprè (1854) and the *Nicolò Machiavelli* by Lorenzo Bartolini (1846) they are quite mediocre artworks. On Via della Ninna (the street running between Palazzo Vecchio and the Uffizi), incorporated into the Uffizi's ground floor, are remains of the 11th century Romanesque church, San Piero Scheraggio, that was practically all torn down to make way for the Uffizi. Beneath the archway leading to Via Lambertesca is Buontalenti's *Porta delle Suppliche* (where clemency pleas were left), above which is a bust of Cosimo I.

At the beginning of Via Lambertesca, on the left side, is a restored tower-house, the Pulci Palace. It is now the headquarters of the **Accademia dei Georgofili,** a centuries

66

old foundation for furthering agricultural studies, which boasts an extensive library on the subject. Retracing our steps to the *Piazzale degli Uffizi*, one of the last doors along the west arcade (Uffizi entrance side) is the entranceway to the **State Archives.** Spreading over more than 400 rooms, the archives contain one of the greatest collections of historical documents and manuscripts in all Italy, as well as a library specializing in Florentine and Tuscan history. In the exhibition hall is a display featuring the *"Fiorinaio"* (the register kept by the Florentine mint) with stamp impressions of all the gold and silver coins the city minted between 1318 and 1858, the *Edict of Union of the Greek and Latin churches* (1439), the *Libro del Chiodo* which records the sentencing of a number of Ghibelline figures (rivals of the Guelphs), one of whom was Dante himself. In addition, there are various edicts, diplomas, nautical maps, parchments, 4th-6th century B.C. papyrus rolls, and autographs of famous humanist figures, Medici princes, and foreign personages. Leaving the Archives we return towards Palazzo Vecchio, and re-entering the building between the niche statues of *Cosimo il vecchio "Pater Patriae"* (Cosimo the Elder, father of his country) and *Lorenzo the Magnificent* on the same side of the arcade, we find ourselves inside the Uffizi Gallery.

67

Uffizi - The first wing. In Vasari's original construction this was part of a long loggia which topped the building. Today it contains a superb exhibit of tapestries and sculpture, including Classical sarcophagi.

THE UFFIZI GALLERY

THE UFFIZI GALLERY — The basic collection of the renowned museum consists mainly of masterpieces of Tuscan—and especially Florentine—painting of the 13th through 16th centuries. There are also outstanding works of the other major Italian schools, e.g. Umbrian, Emilian, Venetian, not to mention Flemish, French, and German paintings of great note. It is easy to see why the Uffizi ranks as the foremost museum in Italy and one of the greatest in the world. The original core of the museum comprised the private collections of the Medicis and the Lorraine granddukes.

It was actually Francesco I dei Medici, a great art connoisseur in his own right, who in 1574 commissioned the architect Buontalenti to remodel the original loggia on the second floor so that the treasures, then in Palazzo Vecchio and scattered among the grandducal possessions, collected by Cosimo the Elder, Lorenzo the Magnificent, and his own father, Grandduke Cosimo I, could be admired in rooms especially designed for that purpose. In 1610 Buontalenti was again commissioned, this time by Ferdinando I, to design the so-called *"tribuna"* so that Ferdinando could fittingly

display the works he had collected in the Villa Medici in Rome. Ferdinando II added on new rooms to house the works he had acquired through the Della Rovere bequest, while at the same time Cardinal Leopoldo was busy setting up his own collection of self-portraits and prints and drawings. Cosimo III donated gemstones, medals, and coins, and also had a number of well-known statues brought up from Rome, among which the Medici Venus, the Knife-grinder, and the Wrestlers. When Giangastone de' Medici died, the last of the great dynasty, Anna Maria Lodovica, wife of the Palatine Elector, who had already enriched the precious collection with Flemish and German masterpieces, bequeathed the whole gallery to the Italian state. She made one condition however (the "Family Pact" of 1737); the collection has to remain forever in Florence. The Medicis' successors, the Lorraine grandukes, continued the tradition of enriching this artistic patrimony. Francesco II of Lorraine donated classical pieces and coins. Pietro Leopoldo, not only reunited the Medici collections still scattered about Rome and Florence, but also had the famous statues of Niobe and her

69

children brought from the Villa Medici in Rome and set up in a room expressly designed to show them off. Unfortunately, heavy losses were suffered when Napoleon's troops rampaged through Italy carying off art works as spoils of war, but most of these were later recovered. The present arrangement of the museum dates from the postwar period and was conceived in accordance with the most up-to-date museum criteria.

Just past the ticket counters, we follow the raised platform, on either side of which are Andrea del Castagno's renowned frescoes of *Famous Men*. Originally painted for the Villa Pandolfini in nearby Legnaia (15th century), they are representations of well-known literary, mythological, and historical figures, from right to left: the Cuman Sibyl, Boccaccio, Petrarch, Dante, Farinata degli Uberti, Pippo Spano, Queen Esther, and Queen Tomiri. This hall and the following one, once part of the church of **San Piero Scheraggio,** have been recently restored. The second hall, on the site of the church's apse, contains traces of the original decoration as well as works by 14th century Tuscan painters. Sandro Botticelli's splendid *Annunciation* graces the hall off to the right. The impressive staircase leading to the upper floors, designed by Vasari, is decorated with sculptures of various periods, many of which are Roman copies of Greek originals. Off the second floor landing is the entrance to the **Gabinetto dei disegni e delle stampe** (Prints and Drawings Collection). This unique collection, started by Cardinal Leopoldo de' Medici, now comprises over 100,000 pieces by Italian and foreign artists. The vestibule with antique statues on the third floor leads to the first wing of the actual museum.

FIRST WING – The first gallery is the spacious loggia that Buontalenti remodeled by order of Francesco I. On either side of the corridor are 4th-6th century A.D. Roman sarcophagi, as well as Roman busts and statues. The walls are hung with exquisite Flemish and Florentine tapestries. The ceiling decoration in the so-called grotesque style is by Allori and other 16th century painters.

ROOM I – (At the beginning of the corridor, generally closed) Roman and Greek sculpture.

ROOM II – This is the hall of the 13th century Italian school. The works displayed here give the observant spectator a splendid chance to perceive how and when Italian painting started to break away from the stiffer, more schematic Byzantine tradition. The forerunners of what would be called the "Renaissance style" are Cimabue, here represented by a superb *Virgin enthroned and angels,* Duccio di Buoninsegna from Siena with his *Rucellai Madonna* (originally painted for the Rucellai Chapel in the Santa Maria Novella Church), and perhaps the most revolutionary of all, Giotto, whose unique *Virgin enthroned* is the first work that greets your eye upon entering the room. Generally dated 1303-1305, when Giotto was reputedly working on a fresco cycle in Assisi, this painting's naturalistic style (e.g. the realistic approach to space and architecture) is already a far cry from the schematic icon-like figures flatly silhouetted against gold ground typical of its Byzantine counterparts. In addition, there are works by 13th century artists from the school of Lucca: *St. Francis receiving the Stigmata,* a diptych with the *Virgin and Child surrounded by saints,* and a *Crucifixion* from the school of Bonaventura Berlinghieri. Also noteworthy are *St. Luke the Evangelist* by the Magdalen Master, the *Savior amidst the Virgin and saints* by Meliore di Jacopo, and a *Crucifix with scenes of the Passion,* Pisan school 12th century.

ROOM III – This room is filled with splendid examples of the especially refined style that typified 14th century Sienese art. They include major works by the Lorenzetti brothers, two of the foremost Sienese artists of the period: Ambrogio's *Circumcision of Christ* and *scenes from the life of St. Nicholas* and Pietro's *scenes from the life of the Blessed Humility* and *Sts. John, Mark,* and *Luke.* Perhaps the highlight amongst such treasures is Simone Martini's *Annunciation,* a veritable masterpiece of lyrical grace and refinement expressed through curving line and glowing color. In addition, there is a *Virgin and Child* by Niccolò di Sozzo Tegliacci, a *Nativity* by Simone de' Crocifissi, and a *Presentation at the Temple* by Niccolò Bonaccorsi.

ROOM IV – This room is dedicated to 15th century Florentine painters, especially followers of Giotto. These include Bernardo Daddi's *Virgin and Child* and *Virgin and Child with saints* (two of the latter subject), Nardo di Cione's *Crucifixion,* Taddeo Gaddi's *Virgin in Glory,* and Giottino's lovely *Pietà.*

Uffizi - Virgin enthroned by Giotto.

Uffizi - Annunciation by Simone Martini (detail).

ROOMS V-VI — The paintings here are typical examples of late 14th-early 15th century Italian painting. This particular blend of Giottoesque earthiness, Sienese refinement, plus a great profusion of elaborate ornamentation is known as the International Style, the so-called "flowery Gothic." The foremost International style painters are represented here: Gentile da Fabriano (*Adoration of the Magi* and *Four Saints*), Lorenzo Monaco (the huge *Coronation of the Virgin* and another *Adoration of the Magi*), Gherardo Starnina (the *Thebaid*), Agnolo Gaddi (*Crucifixion*), and Giovanni di Paolo (*Virgin and Child with saints*). The three panels depicting *scenes from the life of St. Benedict* are by an unknown Northern Italian artist.

ROOM VII — This room contains several famous masterpieces of 15th century painting. These are: *Coronation of the Virgin* and *Virgin and Child* by Fra Angelico, *Virgin and Child surrounded by Saints* by Domenico Veneziano, and the *Virgin and St. Anne* by Masaccio and Masolino (Masaccio's teacher). In the middle of the floor are the *portraits of Battista Sforza and Federico da Montefeltro,* painted by Piero della Francesca, on the back of which are allegorical triumphs of the Duke and Duchess. A whole wall is taken up by Paolo Uccello's *Battle of San Romano* which once hung in Lorenzo the Magnificent's bedroom in the Medici-Riccardi Palace.

ROOM VIII — Here are 15th century paintings, mostly by Fra Filippo Lippi (a predella strip of *St. Fregidian deviating the Serchio River;* the *Annunciation of the death of the Virgin;* St. Augustine in his study; the *Coronation of the Virgin,* which features fine portraits of several of Lippi's contemporaries; an altarpiece with the *Annunciation and saints;* the charming *Virgin and Child and two angels;* an *Adoration of the Babe*

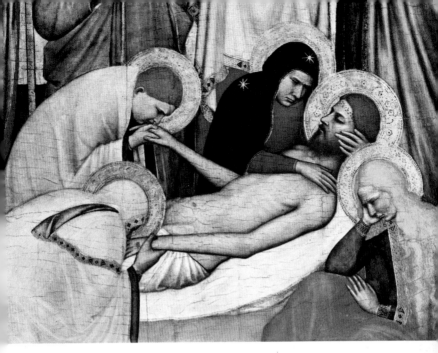

Uffizi - *Above:* "Pietà" by Giottino (detail); *below:* Adoration
of the Magi by Gentile da Fabriano (detail).

Uffizi - Virgin and Child with St. Anne by Masolino and Masaccio.

with St. Ilarion; and another *Adoration with Sts. John and Romualdus*). Other painters represented are Alessio Baldovinetti (*Annunciation* and *Virgin and Child surrounded by saints*), Lorenzo Vecchietta (*Virgin enthroned*), and Nicholas Fromenti (triptych depicting the *Resurrection of Lazarus*).

ROOM IX — The seated figures of *Virtues* are by Antonio Pollaiolo, except for *Strength* which is by Botticelli. Antonio and Piero Pollaiolo, two brothers, both worked on the fine portrait of *Galeazzo Sforza.* The *portrait of a youth with the red beret* is by Filippino Lippi, son of Filippo and pupil of Botticelli.

ROOMS X-XIV — This area is mostly devoted to works by the great master of line and color, Sandro Botticelli whose curving line and pastel tones came to typify Florentine painting of the entire second half of the 15th century. Some of his most famous paintings are hanging here: the *Birth of Venus* and the *Allegory of Spring,* both impregnated with symbolic meaning; the *Madonna del Magnificat;* the *Calumny;* the *Annunciation;* the *Adoration of the Magi* and the *portrait of a young man with a medallion.* The room also contains noteworthy works by Roger Van der Weyden, Ghirlandaio, Filippino Lippi, and last, but far from least, Hugo Van der Goes' superb *Portinari Altarpiece.*

Uffizi - Tribune.

ROOMS XV and XVI — The latter is known as the Map Room from the maps of Tuscany frescoed on the walls by Buonsignori. However, these rooms are generally closed to the public.

ROOM XVII — This room is entered by way of the so-called "Tribune." Important works by Andrea Mantegna are on display: the *Adoration of the Shepherds,* the *Circumcision,* the *Madonna delle Cave.* Of equal note are two Hellenistic sculptures: *Amor and Psyche* and the famous *Sleeping Hermaphrodite* (2nd century B.C.).

ROOM XVIII — The **"Tribune"** was designed by Buontalenti c. 1589 as a showcase for the Medici's most treasured pieces. Standing in the middle is the renowned *Medici Venus,* a Greek masterpiece of the 3rd century B.C. The walls are hung with 16th century portraits by several of the best-known Mannerist painters (16th century). Two female portraits by Bronzino are especially handsome — *Eleonora di Toledo* and *Lucrezia Panciatichi.* There are also fine paintings by Rosso Fiorentino, Vasari, and Carlo da Verona, not to mention the many pieces of Greek and Roman sculpture, inlaid furniture, and a mother-of-pearl dome which complete the decorative scheme.

Uffizi - Birth of
Venus by Botticelli.
It was painted in
1486 for Pierfrancesco
de' Medici for his
villa at Castello.

Uffizi - Allegory of
Spring by Botticelli.
It was painted in
1478 and was also
commissioned by
Pierfrancesco de'
Medici.

Uffizi - Virgin and Child by Luca Signorelli; *right:* **Holy Family by Michelangelo.**

ROOM XIX — The paintings in this room come from the Central Italian schools, including outstanding works by Perugino (portraits and a *Virgin between Sts. John the Baptist and Sebastian*) and by Luca Signorelli (the *Holy Family Tondo,* and a *Virgin and Child,* two of Signorelli's finest paintings). There is also a lovely *Annunciation* by Melozzo da Forli and works by two painters greatly influenced by Perugino, Lorenzo Costa and Gerolamo Genga.

ROOM XX — Devoted to the German school, the room contains several well-known paintings by one of the school's major representatives, Dürer: the *Calvary* (next to it is Brueghel's copy), portraits of *St. James the Greater* and *St. Philip the Apostle,* the *Adoration of the Magi, Portrait of the Artist's Father,* and a *Virgin and Child.* The *Portraits of Luther and His Wife, Luther and Melanchthon,* and *Adam and Eve* are by Lucas Cranach. Other works by 16th century German masters complete the series.

ROOM XXI — The room is devoted to the 15th century Venetian school with an emphasis on Giorgione and Giovanni Bellini. The latter is represented by a *portrait of a gentleman, Sacred Allegory* whose esoteric symbolism is made even more mysterious by the daylight setting, and the *Lamentation of Christ.* Giorgione's works are *Moses before Pharaoh* and the *Judgment of Solomon.* There are also paintings by other well-known Northern Italian artists: the *Warriors and the Old Men,* by Carpaccio, *St. Louis of Toulouse* by Bartolomeo Vivarini, *Christ in the Temple* by Giovanni Mansueti, the delicate *Virgin and Child* by Cima da Conegliano, and *St. Dominic* by Cosmè Tura.

ROOM XXII — This room is devoted to Northern Renaissance painters, among whom Hans Holbein, the great portrait painter (*Self-portrait and Portrait of Sir Richard Southwell*), Gerard David (the dramatic *Adoration of the Magi*), Lukas van Leyden (*Christ crowned with thorns*) and Albert Altdorfer (*Life of St. Florian*).

ROOM XXIII — This room is devoted to Antonio Allegri, better known as Correggio (1489-1534), who was greatly influenced by Leonardo. Correggio's hallmark, soft color and no contours, is evident in the works displayed here (the *Virgin in Glory,* the *Rest on the Flight to Egypt,* and the *Adoration*). Other works by Northern Italian painters influenced by Leonardo are also exhibited.

ROOM XXIV — Generally closed to the public, this room contains Italian and foreign miniatures from the 15th to 18th centuries.

SECOND WING — This section connects the two main corridors of the Uffizi. The works displayed are Roman sculptures. Noteworthy are the *Boy removing a thorn from his foot, Venus,* two *Roman matrons,* and the *Girl preparing for the dance.*

THIRD WING — This corridor too is decorated with some fine Roman sculptures, mainly dating from the 2nd through the 4th century A.D. At the beginning are two statues of *Marsyas flayed* (the one on the right was retouched by Donatello). Farther on are a *Discus-thrower, Leda and the Swan,* and other statues of personages from Greek mythology. Along the walls is a set of Flemish *tapestries with scenes from the life of Christ.*

ROOM XXV — Displayed here among other masterpieces of 16th century painting is one of Michelangelo's rare panel paintings, the so-called *Doni Tondo,* commissioned by Angelo Doni. The subject is the Holy Family. There is also a *portrait of Perugino,* attributed to Raphael, as well as works by Rosso Fiorentino and Albertinelli, two well known Tuscan Mannerists.

ROOM XXVI — This is the Raphael room: the famous *Madonna del Cardellino, Leo X with Cardinals Giulio de' Medici and Luigi de' Rossi, Self-portrait* (on an easel), and *Portrait of Francesco Maria della Rovere* are all to be found here. In addition, there is an outstanding work by the Renaissance master, Andrea del Sarto — dubbed "the painter without error" — called the *Madonna delle Arpie* (Virgin of the Harpies), not to mention fine works by Mannerists such as Pontormo (the *Martyrdom of St. Maurice*) and several portraits.

ROOM XXVII — This room is devoted to two of the foremost 16th century Mannerist painters, Bronzino and Pontormo. The *Holy Family, Lamentation of Christ,* and refined *Portrait of a lady* are by Bronzino, whereas the *Supper at Emmaus,* the *Birth of St. John the Baptist, Portrait of a musician, Portrait of Maria Salviati,* and the *Virgin and saints* were painted by Pontormo. There are also works by Franciabigio and Rosso Fiorentino.

ROOM XXVIII — This room is devoted to Titian (1477-1576) whose rich palette and emphatic use of light and shade became the hallmark of the Venetian school. Perhaps the best-known are the *Venus of Urbino,* the *Flora,* the *Portraits of Eleonora Gonzaga,* and *Francesco Maria della Rovere,* duke and duchess of Urbino, and *Venus and Cupid.* A follower of Titian's, Palma il Vecchio, painted the *Resurrection of Lazarus,* the *Sacra Conversazione,* and *Judith.*

ROOM XXIX — Several of Parmigianino's (1505-1540) finest works are hanging here: the *Virgin and Child with saints,* a *Portrait of an unknown gentleman,* and the magnificent *Madonna dal Collo Lungo* (the Virgin with the long neck). Other artists represented are Ludovico Mazzolino, Luca Cambiaso, Scarsellino, and Girolamo da Carpi.

ROOM XXX — The painters whose works are displayed here belong to the Central Italian Emilia-Romagna school. Mazzolino is represented by the *Circumcision of Christ* and the *Virgin and St. Anne.*

Uffizi - Madonna del Cardellino by Raphael.

ROOM XXXI — Among the works displayed are several by Dosso Dossi, a Ferrarese artist greatly influenced by the Venetian school: *Portrait of a soldier,* the *Virgin in Glory,* and *Witchcraft.* Paintings by 16th century Venetians such as Lorenzo Lotto and Sebastiano del Piombo are also displayed.

ROOM XXXII — This room contains works by a prominent Venetian artist, Sebastiano del Piombo (1485-1547), known for his skillful modeling of luminous color into form. A fine example is the *Death of Adonis* hanging here, by many considered his masterpiece. In addition, works by Lorenzo Lotto (*Sacra Conversazione, Susanna and the Elders*) and Paris Bordone (two portraits) are exhibited.

ROOM XXXIII — Also known as the "16th Century Hall" this passageway is hung with late 16th century Italian and foreign works including François Clouet's *Portrait of Francis I,* Alessandro Allori's *Portrait of Torquato Tasso,* Bronzino's *Allegory of Happiness,* and Jacopo Ligozzi's *Three Ages of Man.*

Uffizi - Adoration of the Magi by Leonardo da Vinci.

ROOM XXXIV — This room is devoted to Paolo Caliari better known as Veronese (1528-1588), one of the foremost 16th century Venetian school painters. Displayed are his *St. Agatha crowned by angels,* the *Martyrdom of St. Justine,* the *Annunciation,* and the *Holy Family.* Other artists whose works hang here include Giulio Campi and Giovanni Battista Moroni, two prominent 16th century portrait painters.

ROOM XXXV — Here one can admire important works by Tintoretto (1518-1594) whose style is a combination of startling light and shade contrasts emphasizing intensely animated composition. The result is a uniquely dramatic effect that is typified in the *Good Samaritan,* the *Apparition of St. Augustine, Leda, Portrait of Jacopo Sansovino,*

Uffizi - The Corridoio Vasariano.

and *Portrait of a red-headed man.* The *Story of Joseph, Annunciation to the Shepherds,* and *Portraits of the artist* are by another renowned 16th century Venetian artist, Jacopo Bassani. In addition, there are works by Federico Barocci and El Greco.

From Room XXXV you go directly to Room XLI as Rooms XXXVI to XL were eliminated when the newly-restored *Scala di Buontalenti* (staircase designed by Buontalenti) was re-opened.

ROOM XLI — Works by the Flemish masters Rubens and Van Dyck are displayed here. Rubens' (1577-1640) impressive canvases of *Henry IV's triumphal entrance into Paris* and *Henry IV at the Battle of Ivry,* as well as two of his portraits, one of his wife *Isabel* and one of the *Emperor Charles V,* are splendid examples of the Fleming's exuberant style. Anthony Van Dyck's portaits are rendered with incomparable skill, as is Susterman's *Portrait of Galileo.*

ROOM XLII — Here, in addition to the famous group of *Niobe and her children* (Roman copies of a Hellenistic Greek work), you find masterpieces of various periods, from Leonardo's *Annunciation* and unfinished *Adoration of the Magi* (16th century) to Canaletto's *Views of Venice* (18th century).

ROOM XLIII — Although this room primarily offers important examples of Flemish and Dutch school paintings (ranging from Ruysch to Van Mieris) the superb *seascape* is by the French master, Claude Lorrain.

ROOM XLIV — Three extraordinary canvases by the unequaled master of light and shade, Caravaggio (1573-1610), are here: the *Medusa, Bacchus,* and the *Sacrifice of Isaac.* In addition, there are paintings by the landscapist, Salvator Rosa, and Giuseppe Maria Crespi.

The **"Corridoio Vasariano" (Vasari's Corridor).** The *"corridoio"* (entrance from the beginning of the third wing) is actually a long raised passageway connecting the Uffizi building to the Pitti Palace by way of Ponte Vecchio. On both sides are famous self-portraits: just to mention the best-known you see those of Leonardo, Titian, Vasari, Palma the Younger, Veronese, Rosalba Carriera, Correggio, Guido Reni, Pompeo Batoni, Rubens, Rembrandt, Van Dyck, Dürer, and Velasquez.

Midway along the third wing is the museum exit preceded by a vestible in which there are two superb Goyas and the Hellenistic bronze *Wild Boar,* a copy of which has been placed in the Straw Market.

THIRD ITINERARY

Piazza della Repubblica - Loggia del Mercato Nuovo - Via Por Santa Maria - Ponte Vecchio - Via Guicciardini - Palazzo Pitti (Palatine Gallery; Gallery of Modern Art; Royal Apartments; Carriage Museum; Silver Museum; Boboli Gardens) - Via Romana - Via Maggio - Church of Santo Spirito - Church of Santa Maria del Carmine (Brancacci Chapel).

Piazza della Repubblica — This square has been the center of the city life ever since the late 19th century when the old city center then on the site was torn down as a sanitary measure. Today open-air cafes and fine shops line the square and the streets leading to it. On the far side, west of the triumphal arch, the southern arcade brings you right to the main post office building.

The Straw Market (Loggia del Mercato Nuovo) — Via Calimala just off Piazza Repubblica leads right to the Straw Market, the Renaissance loggia of graceful arches on a raised platform designed by Giovanni del Tasso (1547-1551). Once long ago

The Loggia del Mercato Nuovo (Straw Market) - *Left:*
Piazza della Repubblica.

the loggia served as Florence's bustling silk and gold trade center but nowadays people come here to buy straw, embroidery, lace, and other typical wares created by Florentine craftsmen. On the south side is a fountain with a statue of a wild boar on it known as "*il porcellino*" (piglet). The boar is a 17th century copy (by Pietro Tacca, 1612) of the Greek original in the Uffizi.

On Via di Capaccio, just off the marketplace, is a lovely early 14th century palace, the **Palazzo di Parte Guelfa.** Remodeled and enlarged at the beginning of the 15th century by Brunelleschi, who also designed the façade, it was completed in the 16th century by Giorgio Vasari who added on the elegant loggia. Inside on the second floor there is a huge Brunelleschi-style hall with a wooden ceiling designed by Vasari and a Luca della Robbia glazed *terracotta* in the lunette.

Retracing our steps we reach Via Porta Rossa (on the arcade side of the street), going left down it until we come to Piazza Davanzati, just a few yards from the arcade. On the square are two important medieval buildings, the **Palazzo Davanzati,** a typical 14th century palace, and the **Foresi Tower,** one of the few extant of the over 150 tower-houses which were used for defense in 13th century Florence.

Via Por Santa Maria – Passing the Straw Market in the direction of the Arno, we reach Via Por Santa Maria, bombed in World War II, and completely reconstructed. Towards the end of the street, on the lefthand side is a tiny square. The green and white marble façade of the church of **Santo Stefano and Santa Cecilia** built in 1233 is typical of the Tuscan Romanesque style, although the interior was remodeled in the 17th century by Pietro Tacca. The building, partially damaged during the war, has been extensively restored. Back in Via Por Santa Maria, on the opposite side, are two 11th and 13th century tower-houses, one of which the **Torre degli Amidei,** with its two lion-head brackets, is of especial note. Having reached the end of Via Por Santa Maria, we are now before the most famous bridge in the world, Ponte Vecchio.

PONTE VECCHIO — This bridge is called *"vecchio"* (old) because, from Etruscan times on, there has always been a crossing here. The first documented wooden construction dating back to 972 was washed away in the 1333 flood. It was rebuilt in stone in 1345 by Neri di Fioravante who endowed it with its best known feature, the row of shops on either side. Originally, though, these were butcher shops until the 16th century when Cosimo I evicted the butchers and let the shops to silver and goldsmiths, who are still here today. Along the left side runs the famed *"Corridoio Vasariano"* (Vasari's Corridor) which connects the Uffizi and the Pitti Palace. Halfway down the bridge is a modern bust of Benvenuto Cellini by Raffaele Romanelli (1900). There is a magnificent view of the Santa Trinita Bridge from the statue side and a splendid panorama of Piazzale Michelangelo and San Miniato from the Corridor side.

Ponte Vecchio - *Left:* **Romanelli's bust of Benvenuto Cellini.**

Via Guicciardini – This attractive thoroughfare is the street leading from Ponte Vecchio to the Pitti Palace. Just a few yards beyond the bridge is a tiny square off the street, Piazza Santa Felicita, once the site of a 5th century oratory and an Early Christian cemetery. The **church of Santa Felicita** now on the spot, though very old, was rebuilt a number of times. Ferdinando Ruggeri gave it its present appearance in the 18th century. In the first chapel to the left of the entrance designed by Brunelleschi is an extraordinary *Deposition* by Pontormo (1528). In the elegant square-shaped sacristy (1470) designed by a follower of Brunelleschi's there are several noteworthy paintings such as a *Virgin and Child with saints,* an altarpiece by Taddeo Gaddi, and *Santa Felicita and her seven children,* a panel painting with a gold ground by Neri di Bicci. Also, in the adjoining semi-circular chapel, there is a *Crucifixion* panel by Giovanni del Biondi. At the end of Via Guicciardini, on the lefthand side, is an impressive mansion, **Palazzo Guicciardini,** for over five hundred years home of the famous Guicciardini family. It was built in the 15th century and remodeled in the 1600s. The street terminates at Piazza Pitti, the huge square which serves as an appropriate setting for the magnificent Pitti Palace.

Piazza Pitti - The square is embraced by the three wings of the Pitti Palace. The central core of the building was put up around 1450 for the Pitti family (rivals of the Medicis).

PALAZZO PITTI — The most monumental of Florence's stately mansions, the Pitti Palace was built to Brunelleschi's design in the mid 1400s. It was commissioned by a rival of the Medici family, the wealthy merchant, Luca Pitti. He wanted his to be the biggest palace of all and demanded that the windows be as large as the portal to the Medici Palace on Via Larga (later known as the Medici-Riccardi Palace on Via Cavour). Brunelleschi designed the core of the building we see today. Three storeys high, Brunelleschi's simple but harmonious rusticated stone rectangle is an example of perfect equilibrium achieved in spatial terms. Work on Brunelleschi's design progressed steadily until 1465 when the Pitti family went bankrupt. In 1549 the building was bought by Cosimo I's wife, Eleanor of Toledo who commissioned Bartolomeo Ammannati to finish it up.

Ammannati was able to carry out his task, without altering Brunelleschi's original design to any great extent, during the years 1558-1570. Thereafter in 1620 the façade was extended on either side under the supervision of Giulio Parigi. In 1640 Giulio's son, Alfonso, further enlarged it to its present size. The lateral wings (known as "*rondò*") designed by Giuseppe Ruggeri were added on in the years 1764-1783. The great palace, once the residence of the Medici and Lorraine families, was inhabited by Italy's royal family, the Savoys, during the brief period (1865-1871) that Florence was capital of the newborn Kingdom of Italy. Today it houses famous museums— the Palatine Gallery, the Silver Museum, and the Gallery of Modern Art, to name the most important. Special exhibitions are often held here.

Palazzo Pitti - Courtyard.

THE COURTYARD — The main doorway leads into the imposing 16th century court-yard designed by Ammannati (1558-1570). It makes an incomparable setting for the **Artichoke Fountain** designed by Antonio Susini and Francesco Ferrucci the Younger, known as Tadda, at the end of the 16th century. Only three of the four sides of the courtyard are complete; the fourth side makes up the terrace adorned with two little fountains (Hercules and Anteus on the left, Hercules on the right). The door in the middle leads to a grotto, the 17th century **Moses Grotto,** decorated with allegorical statues. Taking the stairway on the right side of the courtyard or, as we recommend, the elevator, to the third floor, we begin our tour at the Gallery of Modern Art.

The Gallery of Modern Art — Founded by the Tuscan provisional government in 1860, this museum contains a fascinating collection of Italian 19th century artworks. In addition to the neo-Classical and academic schools profusely represented, there are also numerous paintings of the so-called *"macchiaiolo"* ("spot") school, a Tuscan movement which up to now has been pretty much ignored by non-Italian art historians. Yet this movement, in many ways akin to French Impressionism, was quite a break with tradition. The "macchiaioli" artists strived to free themselves from the restrictions and conventions of academic art, looking for their inspiration in a direct personal contact with nature and reality. Works by the head of the movement, Giovanni Fattori, and all of its major exponents, Silvestro Lega, Telemaco Signorini, Giuseppe Abbati, Raffaele Sernesi, may be viewed. There are also works by contemporary living artists.

The Coach Museum — (The entrance is under the arcade of the right wing of the palace). This fascinating little museum contains the actual carriages in use from the 16th through 19th centuries, as well as fittings and costumes dating from various periods. In the entrance hall are precious fittings that once belonged to the Medicis and the Savoys, the Italian royal family. In addition there are prints showing costumes of the Medici court of the last period (18th century). The second room contains the exhibition of coaches, among which is the sedan belonging to the last grandduchess of Tuscany, Maria Luisa (18th century); the coaches belonging to the Duke of Modena, Francesco II (17th century); the Granddduke of Tuscany, Leopoldo II (1815); the King of Naples, Ferdinando (1839); Caterina de' Medici (16th century); as well as the special chair Granddduke Cosimo II used for going up and down stairs, since his legs were paralyzed.

Returning to the courtyard, we go up to the second floor of the palace and enter the Palatine Gallery.

THE PALATINE (OR PITTI) GALLERY — The collection numbers over 500 paintings, many of which are well-known masterpieces, and superb collections of precious *objets d'art* which are not only living proof of the fabulous wealth of the Medici family, but also reveal the Medicis' ingrained love of the arts. In fact, it was due to the Medicis—who collected works and patronized artists in every art, major and minor, with such great passion and taste generation upon generation—that Florence became the world's art center for hundreds of years. The original core of the collection was put together by Cosimo II (1620). Later, under Ferdinando II, it was enriched by the treasures brought from Urbino by Ferdinando's wife, Vittoria della Rovere, The granddukes who followed Ferdinando, both Medici and Lorraine, continued in this tradition. The arrangement of such a huge number of paintings, seemingly haphazardly piled up in their elaborately decorated rooms, is simply a reflection of the decorative taste of the past.

The staircase, in the style of Brunelleschi, was designed by Luigi del Moro in 1897. It leads to a vestibule adorned with a fountain attributed to Francesco Ferrucci, surmounted by a statue of a *Boy with a goose* by Tribolo. On the first floor we cross a vestibule and gallery to reach, on the left side, the Dining or Niche Room. From here, turning left again, we enter the Royal Apartments, and to the right, the Palatine Gallery.

SALA DI VENERE (Venus Room) — The ceiling was frescoed by Pietro da Cortona and Ciro Ferri and adorned with exquisite stuccowork by Roman artists (1641-1642). Several extraordinary paintings are hanging here, including Titian's renowned *"La Bella"*, probably a portrait of Duchess Eleonora Gonzaga from Urbino, a *Sacra Conversazione* by Bonifacio de' Pitati, a *Seascape* by Salvator Rosa, and *Portrait of Pietro Aretino,* one of Titian's late works. In addition, there is another Titian, a *Portrait of Julius II* which is actually a copy of a Raphael, to whom the painting was once attributed as a youthful work. Another of the Titians here, the *Concert,* was once attributed to Titian's master, Giorgione, although it is now widely felt that this is an early work painted when Titian was still greatly under his teacher's influence. There are two Rubens: the *Peasants' return from the fields* and *Ulysses on the Isle of the Phaecians.* Francesco Bassano painted the *Martyrdom of St. Catherine* and Guercino *Apollo and Marsyas.*

SALA DI APOLLO (Apollo Room) — This ceiling fresco is by Pietro da Cortona and Ciro Ferri (1647-1660). The series of great Titians continues here with the *Virgin of the Misericordia* and the *Portrait of the grey-eyed youth.* In addition, there is a superb Tintoretto, *Portrait of Vincenzo Zeno,* as well as *Nymph chased by a satyr* and *St. John the Baptist* by Dosso Dossi, the *Holy Family* and a grandiose *Deposition,* by Andrea del Sarto, a splendid altarpiece by the Mannerist painter Rosso Fiorentino of the *Virgin and saints,* a fine self-portrait by Andrea del Sarto, and lastly a double portrait by Anthony Van Dyck, *Charles I of England and Henry of France.*

Palatine Gallery - Sala di Marte; *right:* **Virgin and Child by Murillo.**

SALA DI MARTE (Mars Room) — The ceiling fresco was again painted by Pietro da Cortona and Ciro Ferri (1646). In addition to two charming versions of the *Virgin and Child* by the Spanish artist, Murillo, there are two major Rubens: a portrait group entitled the *Four Philosophers* (the first standing figure on the left is a self-portrait) and the renowned *Consequences of War,* a huge canvas painted by Rubens in Anvers in 1638. Commissioned by Ferdinando II, the subject was inspired by the bloody Thirty Years' War. Titian is represented by two fine portraits: *Ippolito de' Medici* and *Andrea Vesalio,* Van Dyck by *Portrait of Cardinal Bentivoglio* considered one of his finest, Tintoretto, by *Portrait of Luigi Cornaro,* and Veronese by *Portrait of Daniele Barbaro.* Works by Guido Reni and Guercino complete the exhibition.

SALA DI GIOVE (Jupiter Room) — The mythological scenes on the ceiling are by Pietro da Cortona and Ferri (1643-1645). In the middle of the room is a marble statue of *Victory* by Vincenzo Consani (1867). One of Raphael's best-known paintings, *La Velata* (Lady with a veil) is hanging here. The model who sat for the portrait was probably Raphael's mistress, *la Fornarina* (the baker girl), who often served as his model. There are other fine paintings in the room: Borgognone's *Battle scene,* Andrea del Sarto, *Portrait of the artist and his wife* and a charming *Annunciation* by the same artist, Bronzino's *Portrait of Guidobaldo della Rovere,* Rubens' *Nymphs chased by satyrs,* and Fra Bartolomeo's striking *Deposition.*

Palatine Gallery - Sala dell'Iliade; *right:* **Madonna del Granduca by Raphael.**

SALA DI SATURNO (Saturn Room) — The ceiling fresco by Ferri (1663-1665) is based upon a design by Pietro da Cortona. This room contains a number of Raphael's major works, including the ever popular *Madonna della Seggiola* (Virgin of the Chair), the figures' full, rounded forms denoting the artist's Roman period; *the Portrait of Cardinal Dovizi da Bibbiena;* the unfinished *Madonna del Baldacchino* (Virgin of the Canopy); and the *Wedding portraits of Angelo and Maddalena Doni.* There is also the famous *Madonna del Granduca* of 1505 which was called "of the grandduke" as it was Grandduke Ferdinando III's favorite painting. In the rendering of the scene you can see a subtle blend of Leonardesque and Umbrian influence (Raphael, in fact, grew up in Umbria where he studied under Perugino). Nearby are Perugino's *Deposition* painted in Florence in 1495 and the *Magdalen,* rendered with intense light and shade contrasts. There are also Ridolfo del Ghirlandaio's *Portrait of a goldsmith* and Guercino's *St. Sebastian.*

SALA DELL'ILIADE (Iliad Room) — The ceiling decoration by Luigi Sabatelli portrays episodes from Homer's Iliad. The statue in the middle by Lorenzo Bartolini (1824) represents *Charity.* The highlights of the room are Velasquez's *Equestrian portrait of Philip IV of Spain,* a series of end of the 16th — beginning of the 17th century portraits, of J. Sustermans, the official portrait painter to the Medici court at the time, and a *Portrait of a gentleman* by Titian. There are also an *Assumption* by Andrea del Sarto and Raphael's *Portrait of a lady* known as *La Gravida* (the pregnant woman) painted in Florence when Raphael was still under the influence of Domenico Ghirlandaio.

Palatine Gallery - Death of Lucretia by Filippino Lippi.

SALA DELL'EDUCAZIONE DI GIOVE (Room of the Education of Jupiter) — (To the right off the Sala dell'Iliade). The room was named after the mythological scene of the ceiling fresco by Luigi Catani (1819). The paintings displayed are a striking *Portrait of a man* by Van Dyck, Caravaggio's famous *Sleeping Cupid,* a *Pietà* by Francesco Salviati, and the *Chaste Susanna* by Guercino. The head of Holofernes in Cristoforo Allori's *Judith* is supposedly a self-portrait of the artist.

SALA DELLA STUFA (Room of the Stove) — The walls of this room, which got its name from its position facing the sun, is entirely frescoed by Matteo Rosselli and Pietro da Cortona.

SALETTA DA BAGNO (Bath) — The neo-Classical decorative scheme of stuccowork and bas-reliefs is by Giuseppe Cacialli.

SALA DI ULISSE (Ulysses Room) — The ceiling fresco by Gaspare Martellini depicting *Ulysses' return to Ithaca* was meant to symbolize Ferdinando III's return to Florence and thus the Medici restoration. There are several paintings by the 17th century painter Carlo Dolci (the *Virgin and Child* is especially charming), Cigoli's *Ecce Homo,* Tintoretto's *Portrait of Andrea Frazier,* Filippino Lippi's *Death of Lucretia,* Raphael's *Madonna dell'Impannata* (*impannata*-cloth-refers to the drapery over the window), and a *Portrait of Alfonso di Ferrara* attributed to Titian.

SALA DI PROMETEO (Prometheus Room) — The frescoes on the ceiling and upper section of the wall, by Giuseppe Collignon (1842), depict scenes from the myth of Prometheus. The paintings in the room include Pontormo's *11,000 martyrs,* Albertinelli's *Holy Family* and Luca Signorelli's treatment of the same subject, Filippo Lippi's charming tondo of the *Virgin and Child* and Francesco Botticini's *Virgin and child with angels.*

POCCETTI GALLERY — The room was named after the 16th century painter who frescoed the ceiling. There are two portraits by Rubens, *Ila and the nymphs* by Francesco Furini, the *Martyrdom of St. Bartholomew* by Ribera, four outstanding *landscapes* by Poussin, and the *Missing drachma* by Domenico Feti.

Palatine Gallery - Sala di Ercole.

SALA DELLA MUSICA (Music Room) — It is also known as the Drum Room from the drum-shaped furniture. The table in the middle is made of Russian malachite and has gilded bronze supports.

SALA CASTAGNOLI — The room was named after the painter who decorated it in the 19th century. The huge round *table* in the middle is inlaid with precious stones. Made in Florence in 1851, the top of the table, known as the "Table of the Muses" shows Apollo in his chariot surrounded by symbols of Muses. The bronze support with *Seasons and cupids* is by Giovanni Duprè.

SALA DELLE ALLEGORIE (Allegory Room) — The room is also known as "Sala del Volterrano" (Volterrano is the name of the painter who frescoed the allegorical scenes). The paintings include the *Trick of Pievano Arlotto, Profane Venus,* and *Sleeping Cupid* also by Volterrano, the *Virgin and Child* by Artemisia Gentileschi, as well as *Venus and Amor* and the *Wedding night* by Giovanni da San Giovanni.

SALA DELLE ARTI (Art Room) — The room was frescoed by Podestà in the 19th century. Paintings by Doldi, Ligozzi, and Rustici, and an *Adoration of the Magi* by Cristoforo Allori decorate the walls.

SALA DI ERCOLE (Hercules Room) — Pietro Benvenuti frescoed *Stories of Hercules* in the neo-Classical style. There is also a splendid *Sèvres vase,* a present from Napoleon to Ferdinand III.

SALA DELL'ARCA (Ark Room) — It was frescoed in 1816 by Luigi Ademollo to represent the pavilion David built for the Ark.

CAPPELLA DELLE GRANDUCHESSE (the Chapel of the Grandduchesses, also known as the Reliquary Chapel) — Decorated with gilded stuccowork and frescoes, the chapel was commissioned in the early 17th century by Maria Magdalen of Austria as a private chapel for the use of the grandduchesses.

Palatine Gallery - Dining hall.

The Royal Apartments — These magnificent apartments were the living quarters of the Medicis, the granddukes of Lorraine, and in the 19th century of the Savoys, the Italian royal family.

The first room, the dining room, also called the SALA DELLE NICCHIE (Niches Room), has Medici portraits by Sustermans. There are also exquisite Japanese and Sèvres vases.

SALA VERDE (Green room) is hung with Gobelins tapestries. The allegorical frescoes honoring the Medicis are by Luca Giordano.

SALA DEL TRONO (Throne room) was where the kings of Italy took oath. The room contains portraits by Sustermans and Francesco Porbus, as well as magnificent maiolica vases.

SALA CELESTE (Blue Room) is decorated with Gobelins tapestries, portraits by Sustermans, and rare Chinese vases.

The CHAPEL was turned into a living room after 1865.

Palatine Gallery - Throne room.

The SALA DEI PAPPAGALLI (Parrot Room) was named for the parrot motifs in the tapestries. There are paintings by Titian *(Portrait of the Duchess of Urbino)* and Hans von Aachen *(Portrait of Francesco I)*. This room and the following two make up the living quarters of Margherita, queen of Italy. The SALA GIALLA (Yellow Room), is hung with Gobelins tapestries, as well as portraits, one of which, attributed to J. F. Douven depicts the *Palatine Electress*. The queen's bedroom is furnished with fine Empire-style pieces.

Back in the Sala dei Pappagalli, we enter the suite belonging to King Umberto I. The bedroom, study, and living room are decorated with tapestries and portraits. The SALA DI BONA (Bona Room) was frescoed by Poccetti in the 17th century with scenes showing the *Conquest of the city of Bona in Africa*, the *Conquest of Prevesa, a View of the Leghorn harbor*, and the *Apotheosis of Cosimo I*.

SALA BIANCA (White Room), the ballroom, is adorned with magnificent neo-Classical stuccos and chandeliers. During the reign of the Lorraine granddukes and Savoy monarchs, the room was used for official receptions and ceremonies.

99

A room in the Silver Museum.

After our tour of the Palatine Gallery and the royal apartments, we return to the ground floor for a look at the Silver Museum.

Museo degli Argenti (Silver Museum) — The core of this priceless collection of silver, gemstones, jewels, ivories, porcelain, glassware, and textiles was put together by the Medici family and then further increased by the addition of the Palatine Electress' treasury and bequests by the Savoys and private citizens. Space does not permit us to list each and every object on display; only the highlights will be described.

SALA DI GIOVANNI DA SAN GIOVANNI — Once the antechamber to the granddukes' summer suite, the room was frescoed between 1638 and 1642 by Giovanni di San Giovanni and his pupils. The subject of the frescoes is Lorenzo the Magnificent giving refuge to the Muses after they have been chased from Mt. Parnassus. The ceiling fresco is an allegorical representation of the marriage of Grandduke Ferdinand II to Vittoria della Rovere.

THE CHAPEL — The chapel was frescoed between 1623 and 1634. The 17th century tortoiseshell *crucifix* is noteworthy.

SALA DELL'UDIENZA (Audience Hall) — The frescoes were painted between 1636 and 1641 by the Bolognese artists Colonna and Mitelli. The 17th century ebony *stipo* cabinet inlaid with precious stones was a gift from Archduke Leopold of Tyrol to Ferdinando II in 1628. The ebony prayer stool, also inlaid with precious stones and adorned with a mosaic of the Baptism of Christ, was also crafted in the 17th century.

SALA DELL'UDIENZA PRIVATA (Private Audience Hall) — In this room, also frescoed by Colonna and Mitelli, are five 16th century tables whose tops are adorned with marble and precious stone inlay.

THE THIRD SALA DI RAPPRESENTANZA (Third Audience Hall) — The frescoes are once again by Colonna and Mitelli. In the middle is a late 16th century table with an antique porphyry top and a carved wooden base. Among the other treasures are a *chess set* carved in Florence in 1619, possibly after a design by Jacopo Ligozzi, and the so-called *Stipo dell'Elettore* cabinet which was crafted in the grandducal workshops in 1709 and once belonged to Anna Maria, daughter of Grandduke Cosimo III.

From this room we enter (on the right) a section comprising four rooms. Here displayed in showcases are objects from various schools and periods which are tangible proof of the incredible level the so-called minor arts reached between the 16th and 18th centuries. The highlights include French, German, and Flemish 17th century ivories (especially the ivory *chalices* from Coburg crafted for the Duke of Saxony) several pieces by Balthazar Stockamer, and a 16th century Flemish carved *Crucifixion* once owned by Pope Pius V. In addition, we mustn't overlook the *statuettes of the Apostles* by Orazio Mochi, the *lapis-lazuli vase* crafted for Francesco I de' Medici after a design by Buontalenti, an engraved crystal *goblet* with a gold-plated lid engraved and enameled with the emblems of Henry II of France and Diana of Poitiers, a painting showing *St. Anne teaching the Virgin to read* by Solimena (late 16th-early 17th century), with a fine silver frame, as well as a vast array of reliquaries, cameos, vases, and statuettes.

THE BOBOLI GARDEN — Named after the Boboli Hill on which it rises, this splendid garden is in the so-called Italian style, that is, the landscaping is treated in architectural terms. Eleanor of Toledo, Cosimo I's wife, commissioned Niccolò Pericoli, known as Il Tribolo, to design it in 1542. It was later continued by Ammannati and Buontalenti and completed by Alfonso Parigi.

Turning left, we find the **Fountain of Bacchus.** The model for the rather odd-looking pudgy Bacchus was a dwarf of Cosimo I's entourage. Farther down, opposite the entrance, is the **Grotto of Buontalenti,** a fantastic creation of man-made grottoes, frescoes, sculptures, and fake incrustations. Michelangelo's four Slaves originally intended for Pope Julius II's tomb were once placed in the first grotto; now there are plaster casts in their place. Giambologna's lovely statue of *Venus* is in the third grotto. Returning towards the entrance, a gravel path leads up to the 17th century **Amphitheater** with a gigantic granite basin in the middle moved here from the Baths of Caracalla in Rome and topped by an Egyptian obelisk.

From the Amphitheater we climb the hill to the **Neptune Garden** named after the bronze statue of *Neptune* by Stoldi in the middle of the pool. Turning left here we reach the **Belvedere** which offers a delightful view of the city and the hills of Fiesole. Returning to the giant basin we climb up to the statue of *Abundance* by Giambologna and Tacca. Turning right we reach the **Giardino del Cavaliere** (Knight's Garden) with a fine view of the park. If we take the ramp on the left we come to a pleasant meadow surrounded by cypresses and holmoaks called the **Prato dell'Uccellare.** This is the beginning of the broad path leading to the **Piazzale dell'Isolotto** with Giambologna's *Fountain of Oceanus* in the center. By way of the **Limonaia** (lemon grove) we reach the exit on Via Romana.

Via Romana — The exit of the Boboli Gardens leads right into Via Romana. Before continuing our intinerary (which from here should go right), we shall take a brief excursion to the left. Via Romana comes out at Porta Romana, a massive cropped tower built in 1326. Inside the arch is a fresco by Franciabigio of a *Virgin and Child and four saints.* The road running left of the *piazzale* is the beginning of Viale Machiavelli, a splendid winding drive that skirts the city, passing the panoramic terrace known as Piazzale Michelangelo. The tree-lined road to the right of Viale Machiavelli leads, instead, to the *Villa di Poggio Imperiale,* a very old building which was enlarged by Giulio Parigi in 1620 and later underwent several remodelings. Today it is a private school for girls. Returning to Via Romana, we note a huge fresco depicting *Life in Florence* painted on the upper wall of the first house on the street. It was painted by

Mario Romoli in 1955 to replace a 17th century fresco by Giovanni da San Giovanni no longer extant. Contemporary and historical figures are depicted in a strictly Florentine architectural setting. In the middle above a small window is an *Annunciation*. On the right are the city's famed historical figures: Dante, Giotto, Masaccio, Leonardo, Michelangelo, Savonarola, and Giovanni delle Bande Nere, while on the left we see prominent contemporary Florentines: the writer Giovanni Papini (wearing glasses), the painter (with a self-portrait on the easel), the mathematician Campedelli, the architect Italo Gamberini, and the sculptor Martini (holding a statuette).

Going back to out itinerary, we pick up where we left off at the exit of the Boboli Gardens on Via Romana.

Number 17 Via Romana is the **Specola Natural History Museum** (some yards before the street runs into Piazza San Felice). On the left is the **church of San Felice,** with a façade by Michelozzo (1457) and a fine carved Renaissance portal. The aisleless interior is adorned with several noteworthy paintings: a 14th century *Pietà* by Niccolò di Pietro Gerini (first righthand altar), *Virgin and Child with saints* by

Boboli Gardens - *Left:* **Bacchus Fountain.** *Above:* **Oceanus Fountain.**

Ridolfo del Ghirlandaio (fifth altar), *St. Felix coming to the aid of St. Maximus* by Giovanni da San Giovanni (seventh lefthand altar) and a *Crucifixion* in the choir by a follower of Giotto.

Via Maggio — Via Maggio, the middle street branching out of Piazza San Felice, was actually once called Via Maggiore (Broadway) — indeed it was a very wide street for the times. It is lined with aristocratic mansions built between the 14th and 17th centuries. Number 8, Casa Guidi, is the house that Elizabeth Barrett Browning lived and died in (1861). Over the door is an inscription composed by the Italian writer Niccolò Tommaseo to commemorate her. Number 26, the 16th century Palazzo Buontalenti, was the home of Bianca Cappello, mistress of Francesco de' Medici. There are several other interesting buildings along the way: Number 43, Casa Ridolfi (14th century); Number 50, Casa Rosselli del Turco (15th century); Number 42, Palazzo Corsini (15th century but later remodeled by G. Silvani); and Number 30, Palazzo Biliotti.

Retracing our steps to Piazza San Felice we turn into the sidestreet Via Mazzetta leading to Piazza Santo Spirito, one of Florence's most attractive squares. Number 10 is **Palazzo Guadagni,** an outstanding Florentine Renaissance palace, attributed to Cronaca (1503-1506). The building is surmounted by a graceful loggia and sports a lovely wrought-iron lantern on the corner.

103

Church of Santo Spirito.

THE CHURCH OF SANTO SPIRITO — Santo Spirito was built on the site of a 13th century church, part of an Augustinian monastery. One of the finest of the Early Renaissance buildings, it was begun by Brunelleschi in 1444 and continued by Antonio Manetti and Salvi d'Andrea until its completion in 1487. The graceful belltower on the north side was designed by Baccio d'Agnolo. The dome, designed by Brunelleschi, was put up by Salvi d'Andrea.

THE INTERIOR — The effect of the slender columns and graceful arches along both aisles and the transept is extremely elegant. Once long ago the 38 semi-circular chapels were adorned with art treasures, but many have since been moved elsewhere. Following is a list of the church's major attractions. Right aisle: In the end chapel: a 16th century copy (by Baccio Bigio) of Michelangelo's *Pietà* in St. Peter's. In the 3rd chapel: a wooden statue of *St. Nicolas of Tolentino* attributed to Nanni Ungare. In the 6th chapel: the *Martyrdom of St. Stephen* by Passignano. Behind the Baroque main altar (1608) with an elaborate tabernacle designed by Giovanni Caccini: a wooden *crucifix* attributed to Michelangelo (when he was in his twenties). Right transept: in the 4th chapel on the 15th century altar: a *Virgin and Child with St. John and other saints,* also known as the Tanai Altarpiece from the name of the family that commissioned it, by Filippino Lippi (c. 1490). The elaborate frame is contemporary to the painting. In the 7th chapel behind the bronze grating: the *tomb of Neri Capponi* by Bernardo Rossellino (1458). Apse: in the 1st chapel: a *Virgin with Saints* attributed to Raffaello de' Carli. In the 2nd chapel: a *Virgin and Child with saints* by a pupil of Bernardo Daddi. In the 4th chapel: a painting of *Martyrs* by Alessandro Allori. The predella panel below has a view of Palazzo Pitti before it was enlarged. In the 5th chapel: the *Adultress* also by Alessandro Allori. In the 7th chapel: a 15th century Florentine school *Annunciation* In the 8th chapel: a *Nativity* by a pupil of Ghirlandaio. Left transept: its 15th century appearance is more or less intact. First chapel: *St. Monica founding the Augustinian Order,* a painting by Botticini. 2nd chapel: *Virgin and Child with saints* by Cosimo Rosselli (1482) Fourth chapel: the entire marble ornamentation is an early work by Andrea Sansovino. The railing, dated 1642, is also worthy of note. 5th chapel: *Holy Trinity* by Francesco Granacci. 7th chapel: *Virgin and Child with saints* by Raffaellino del Garbo (1505). 8th chapel: *St. Thomas* by Michele del Ghirlandaio. Left aisle (starting from the left arm of the transept): 1st chapel: *Virgin enthroned with saints* by Fra Bartolomeo, 3rd chapel: *Virgin, St. Anne, and other saints* by Ridolfo and

Church of Santa Maria del Carmine.

Michele del Ghirlandaio, 6th chapel: a copy of Michelangelo's *Christ carrying the Cross* by Taddeo Landini (the original is in Santa Maria sopra Minerva in Rome). At the third bay a door beneath the organ opens into the *vestibule* built by Cronaca in 1494 with barrel vaults resting upon twelve Corinthian columns. The vestibule leads to the lovely octagonal *sacristy* designed by Giuliano da Sangallo.

The Cenacolo (the Last Supper fresco and a small museum) — The entrance is just to the left of the church façade. The collection includes medieval and Renaissance (11th-15th century) sculpture bequeathed to the city by a Florentine art collector, Salvatore Romano.
On the wall of the great hall which once served as the refectory (dining hall) of the Augustinian monks is a huge fresco of the *Last Supper* and the *Crucifixion* by Andrea Orcagna and his helpers (c. 1360). Several detached frescoes dating from the 14th century are also displayed in the hall.

Crossing the square, we turn right into Via Sant'Agostino, cross Via de' Serragli, and continue down Via Santa Monica until we come to Piazza del Carmine.

THE CHURCH OF SANTA MARIA DEL CARMINE — First begun in 1268 in a mixed Romanesque-Gothic style, the church underwent extensive remodeling during the 16th and 17th centuries. In 1771 it was almost completely burnt down in a fire, but miraculously the famous Brancacci and Corsini chapels survived unscathed. Between 1771 and 1775 it was rebuilt by Giuseppe Ruggeri and Giulio Mannaioni in the Baroque style, although the façade was left unfinished as we see it today.

THE INTERIOR — The church has no aisles but chapels along the nave. The ceiling fresco with illusionistic architecture is by Domenico Stagi, whereas the *Ascension* was frescoed by Giuseppe Romei (1780).
In the third righthand altar is a painting by Vasari, *Crucifixion with the Virgin, St. Mary Magdalen, and St. John,* which somehow survived the 1771 fire. At the end of the right transept is the renowned **Brancacci Chapel,** also a survivor of the great fire. The famous frescoes completely covering its walls were commissioned by Felice Brancacci, who also commissioned the erection of the chapel itself. The fresco cycle was begun by Masolino (1424-1425), continued by the great Masaccio (1426-1427)

Santa Maria del Carmine - Tribute Money by Masaccio.

and finished by Filippino Lippi (1484-1485). As Giotto had been in the 14th century, Masaccio was the great innovator of 15th century painting. By using perspective and color rather than line to model forms, he created believable space for his monumental figures. All of the Renaissance masters, Michelangelo and Raphael included, acknowledged their debt to him. Indeed, Masaccio influenced generation upon generation of artists, and this influence has continued up to this day (he accomplished all of this in a very brief time, for Tommaso Guido, nicknamed Masaccio — burly Tom — lived only twenty-eight years, from 1401 to 1428). Before Masaccio, the painter who presumably had been his teacher, Masolino da Panicale, received the commission to fresco the Brancacci family chapel. Masolino was a competent painter but surely no innovator. In fact, the sections painted by him express little more than typical International Style refinement. Abounding in graceful figures, his frescoes stress the storytelling aspect, but he fails to really involve the spectator in what he is telling. Summoned to work in Hungary, Masolino left the Brancacci Chapel to his pupil Masaccio, whose Tribute Money and Expulsion from the Garden of Eden scenes are landmarks in art history. Masaccio, too, was unable to complete the cycle and it was left unfinished until Filippino Lippi managed to conclude it some sixty years later. Lippi tried to live up to his illustrious predecessor, but his work is marred by too much emphasis on narration and attention to details, such as the numerous portrait figures of his contemporaries added to the Biblical scenes. The subjects of the frescoes starting from the upper left side (as you face the altar) are: 1) *Expulsion of Adam and Eve from Paradise* by Masaccio, 2) *Payment of the tribute money* by Masaccio, 3) *St. Peter preaching* by Masolino, 4) *St. Peter baptizing* (on the right of the altar) by Masaccio, 5) the left side of the fresco showing *St. Peter healing the lame man* is by Masaccio while, 6) the right side of *St. Peter raising the dead Tabitha* is by Masolino, 7) *St. Peter in prison* by Filippino Lippi, 9) the left side of the fresco of *St. Peter raising the Emperor's nephew* was begun by Masaccio and finished by Filippino Lippi, 10) the right side with *St. Peter on his throne* is by Masaccio, 11) *St. Peter healing the sick with his shadow* by Masaccio, 12) *St. Peter and St. John distributing alms* by Masaccio, 13) *Sentencing and crucifixion of St. Peter* by Filippino Lippi, and 14) the *angel freeing St. Peter from prison* by Filippino Lippi. The fresco on the chapel ceiling of the *Virgin giving the scapula to the Blessed Simon Stock* was painted by Vincenzo Meucci (1765). The **sacristy** entered from the left side of the Brancacci Chapel is of considerable interest. It contains several 14th and 15th century paintings.

Leaving the church we cross the square at the end of which is Borgo San Frediano, one of the most authentically Florentine streets. Turning left we come to the church of **San Frediano in Cestello,** rebuilt in 1689 by Antonio Ferri.

FOURTH ITINERARY

Piazza del Duomo - Via dei Cerretani - Via Tornabuoni
- Palazzo Strozzi - Piazza Santa Trinita (Church di
Santa Trinita) - Lungarno Corsini (Corsini Gallery) -
Cascine Park - Ognissanti Square and Church -
Piazza Santa Maria Novella (Church and Cloisters
of Santa Maria Novella).

Via dei Cerretani — One of the busiest thoroughfares in the city, this street goes
from Piazza del Duomo to the main railroad station. A few yards from Piazza del
Duomo it passes the **church of Santa Maria Maggiore** (entrance on the little square
around the corner). First built in the 10th century, it was later rebuilt at the end of
the 1200s. Over the portal is a sculpture of the *Virgin and Child* (14th century Pisan
school). Inside is the tomb of *Brunetto Latini,* Dante's master. In the chapel to the
left of the choir is a 13th century painted relief of the *Virgin enthroned* attributed to
Coppo di Marcovaldo. Continuing down Via dei Cerretani, we soon reach the CIT
travel agency where we turn left into Via Rondinelli which in turn leads into Piazza
Antinori.

Piazza Antinori — The square is named for the elegant 15th century **Palazzo degli
Antinori** on the right, attributed to Giuliano da Maiano. Opposite the palace is the
church of San Gaetano. Originally a Romanesque structure, it was entirely rebuilt
in the Florentine Baroque style by Matteo Nigetti, Gherardo and Pier Francesco Silvani.
The aisleless interior is lined in black marble. In the second chapel on the left is the
Martyrdom of St. Lawrence painted by Pietro da Cortona.

Via Tornabuoni — This is Florence's most aristocratic street and one of the most
beautiful in the world. Lining it are lovely old palaces, fine shops, and smart restaurants.
On the right at Number 19 is **Palazzo Larderel,** a lovely late Renaissance building
designed by Giovanni Antonio Dosio (1580). Opposite, at number 20, is **Palazzo
Corsi.** It was remodeled in 1875, although the original construction was designed
by Michelozzo whose elegant inner courtyard is still extant. **Palazzo Viviani,** formerly
Palazzo della Robbia (number 15), was originally the home of the renowned della
Robbia family. It was remodeled in 1639 by G. B. Foggini. At this point Via Tornabuoni
intersects, on the left, Via Strozzi, a busy street leading into Piazza della Repubblica,
while, on our right, two streets, Via della Spada and Via della Vigna Nuova, branch
out in the opposite direction. Midway along Via della Vigna Nuova is the **Loggia dei
Rucellai** designed by Leon Battista Alberti and built in 1468. The loggia was the
setting for the joyous and not so joyous celebrations of the aristocratic Rucellai family.
During the 17th century this unique masterpiece was turned into a shop and apartment
and it remained such until 1963 when the Florentine Tourist Board sponsored a
restoration campaign and made it a tourist information office. The worthy project
was carried out by Prof. Piero Sampaolesi of the Institute for the Restoration of
Monuments. Opposite, at number 18, is **Palazzo Rucellai,** one of the landmarks of
Early Renaissance architecture. The building was put up by Bernardo Rossellino, but
the design, revolutionary with respect to the typical 15th century palace, was Leon
Battista Alberti's (1446-1451). The three storey building is faced with smooth rusticated
stone blocks set off by cornices and pilaster strips and pierced by the traditional two-
part windows. Those interested may ring for the custodian who will open up the
restored **Rucellai Chapel** (around the corner on Via della Spada). Inside is an altarpiece shaped like a temple, called the *Edicola del Santo Sepolcro,* which Leon Battista
Alberti created in colored marble for Giovanni di Paolo Rucellai.

Retracing our steps, we are soon back on Via Tornabuoni, with the majestic Palazzo
Strozzi right before us.

Palazzo Strozzi.

THE STROZZI PALACE — This splendid building ranks as one of the finest Florentine Renaissance buildings. It was begun in 1489 by Benedetto da Maiano who was awarded the commission by Filippo Strozzi, a wealthy merchant and rival of the Medicis. The Medicis had Strozzi exiled from the city but he managed to increase his wealth even more while in exile. Work on the palace was resumed by Simone del Pollaiolo (called "*il Cronaca*") who, despite ten years of toil (1497-1507), left it unfinished. Of extremely elegant appearance, the rusticated stone exterior is framed by a magnificent cornice. The wrought-iron corner lanterns and staffs which add handsome decorative touches to the façade are by Nicolò Grosso known as "*il Caparra*" ("the deposit"). The nickname given to this craftsman, famous for his eccentric ways and capricious nature, derives from the fact that he would never accept a commission, be the client commoner or royalty, without having received advance payment. Hence his nickname, "*caparra.*" The inner courtyard is another superb architectural design by Cronaca.

Continuing down Via Tornabuoni, on the left, is **Palazzo Altoviti** surmounted by a loggia. It was joined to **Palazzo Sangalletti** by a 19th century architect, Silvestri (in 1827). To the right is **Palazzo Giacomini** designed by Gherardo Silvani (17th century) at number 5. Next to it, at number 3, is the 14th century **Palazzo Minerbetti.** At this point, Via Tornabuoni continues beyond **Palazzo Spini-Ferroni,** an austere

Palazzo Spini-Ferroni.

13th century building which still looks like a stronghold. Opposite is another 13th century palace, the elegant **Palazzo Gianfigliazzi.** After this brief stretch, which cannot be said to lack elegant shops, the street runs into the Santa Trinita Bridge.

Piazza Santa Trinita — The Roman granite column in the middle of the square originally came from the Baths of Caracalla in Rome, and was a gift made by Pope Pius IV to Grandduke Cosimo I in 1560. On top is a porphyry statue of *Justice* by Francesco Ferrucci, known as Tadda (1581). On the left at number 2 is **Palazzo Buondelmonti** which belonged to the family that sparked the bitter warring between the Guelph and Ghibelline factions. Number 1 is **Palazzo Bartolini Salimbeni** with its typically Florentine *pietra serena* (a local stone) façade and double row of niche windows. The architect who designed it, Baccio d'Agnolo (1520-1529), was soundly criticized for his great daring in inventing new architectural motifs. He responded by having a Latin inscription engraved on the architrave to the effect that it is easier to criticize something than to imitate it (*"carpere promptius quam imitari"*). Opposite the Bartolini-Salimbeni Palace is the church of Santa Trinita.

Borgo Santi Apostoli, right off Piazza Santa Trinita, is one of the most charming medieval streets in Florence. The towerhouses and palaces along it all date from the 13th and 14th centuries. The restored 11th century **church of Santi Apostoli** is set back on a tiny square midway down the street. The 16th century portal cut into its striking Romanesque façade is a fine work attributed to Benedetto da Rovezzano. The interior has retained its original structure. Over the sacristy door (to the right of the choir) is *the tomb of Bindo Altoviti* surmounted by a statue of *Charity*, attributed to Ammannati. To the left of the main altar is a glazed terracotta *tabernacle* by Andrea della Robbia, and the *tomb of Oddo Altoviti* by Benedetto da Rovezzano (1507). Here, too, is the flint for lighting the sacred fire the day before Easter which according to tradition was brought from the Holy Land by Crusader Pazzino de' Pazzi.

THE CHURCH OF SANTA TRINITA — The church was built
by the Vallombrosan monastic order in the 11th century, although
Niccolò Pisano remodeled it in the 13th century and it was thereafter
enlarged. The Baroque façade was designed by Buontalenti in 1594.
The statue of St. Alexius on the left and the bas-relief depicting
the Trinity on the central portal are by Giovanni Caccini.

THE INTERIOR — This important Gothic church contains equally important art works
of the 14th and 15th centuries. The side chapels were added on in the 14th century.
Upon the inner façade you can see the remains of the original Romanesque church
structure. Right aisle: on the altar of the right chapel *Virgin and Child with saints* by
Neri di Bicci. The fourth chapel was painted by Lorenzo Monaco and has Fra Angelico's
scenes from the life of Mary and *Prophets* on the ceiling. On the altar is a panel painting of the *Annunciation*. In the fifth chapel is a marble altar by Benedetto da Rovezzano.
in the right transept, past the sacristy door, is the *Sassetti Chapel* with the *tomb of
Onofrio Strozzi* by Pietro di Niccolò Lamberti (1421) and a famous *fresco cycle* by
Domenico Ghirlandaio (1483-1486). Outside, on the top, is a fresco with the statue
of David on a painted column. On the right side is the *Tribune Sibyl announcing to
Augustus the birth of Christ.* Inside there are four *sibyls* frescoed on the ceiling and
scenes from the life of St. Francis. Starting from the upper left: 1) *St. Francis giving
up his earthly possessions,* 2) *approval of the Franciscan Rule,* and 3) *the trial by fire
before the sultan.* The lower register starting from the left shows: 4) *St. Francis receiving
the Stigmata,* to the right, 5) *the death of St. Francis;* on the wall behind the altar:
6) *St. Francis, invoked after his death, raises a young man of the Spini family from
the dead.* Below are portraits of Francesco Sassetti and his wife, Nera Corsi, who
commissioned the work. One of Ghirlandaio's best-loved works, the *Adoration of
the Shepherds* (1495), is on the altar. The *tombs of Francesco and Nera Sassetti*
attributed to Giuliano da Sangallo (1491) are here in the chapel.
In the adjoining chapel is a huge *Crucifix.* It is known as the "Crucifix of St.
Giovanni Gualberto" since the painted Christ reputedly nodded his head in approval
when Giovanni knelt in forgiveness before the man who had murdered his brother. The
crucifix is covered by a painting recounting this legend. On the altar of the main chapel

Santa Trinita Bridge - *Left:* **two of the four corner statues.**

is an altarpiece with the *Holy Trinity and saints* by Mariotto di Nardo (1416). The frescoes by Alessio Baldovinetti (c. 1471) on the ceiling are unfortunately in very poor condition. In the left transept in the second chapel to the left of the main one, is an exquisite marble carving by Luca della Robbia, the *tomb of Benozzo Federighi, Bishop of Fiesole.* On the walls are frescoes with *scenes from the life of St. Bartholomew* by Giovanni da Ponte. In the second front chapel is a 15th century Florentine school painting of *Christ's encounter with Mary on the way to Calvary.* Left aisle in the fifth chapel is a charming wooden statue of *Mary Magdalen,* begun by Desiderio da Settignano (1464) and finished by Benedetto da Maiano (1468). In the fourth chapel is a 15th century Sienese school altarpiece with the *Coronation of the Virgin.* A stone plaque indicates the *tomb of Dino Compagni* (1250-1324), Dante's friend and chronicler of his times. The third chapel contains a panel painting by Neri di Bicci of the *Annunciation* set on the altar. The walls are frescoed with the *Disputation of St. Catherine* by followers of Giotto. The Roman sarcophagus with a reclining figure is the *tomb of Giuliano Davanzati.* On the altar of the second chapel·is the *Mystic Marriage of St. Catherine* by Antonio del Ceraiolo (16th century); frescoes by Ridolfo del Ghirlandaio of *St. Jerome in penitence* and the *Annunciation* (1503) are painted on the walls. On request the custodian will open the Romanesque crypt (down the stairs in the middle of the nave) where you can see the remains of the original church.

Ponte Santa Trinita — The first version of the bridge known today as Santa Trinita was designed in 1252 by the two monk-architects who had also designed the church of Santa Maria Novella, Fra Sisto and Fra Ristoro. After its destruction in 1557, Bartolomeo Ammannati, strongly influenced by Michelangelo, designed another bridge to take its place. His design, three flowing arches on sturdy, but elegant pylons, was so successful that Santa Trinita is considered one of the loveliest Renaissance bridges ever built. The statues on the four corners symbolizing the seasons were added in 1608. Destroyed during World War II, the bridge was faithfully reconstructed—stone by stone—by an engineer, Emilio Brizzi, and an architect, Riccardo Gizdulich (1955-1957). A great deal of the building material was recovered from the river and used in the reconstruction.

Lungarno Corsini — This is one of the most attractive stretches of drive along the right bank of the river. It was named after the Corsini, a family numbering several illustrious historical figures among their ancestors—two of these are Lorenzo Corsini (Pope Clement XII, 13th century) and Andrea Corsini, Bishop of Fiesole. Aristocratic palaces line the street. At number 2 is Palazzo Gianfigliazzi (where the British Consulate is located) which was remodeled in the 19th century along with the adjoining building, also the property of the Gianfigliazzi. Number 10 is **Palazzo Corsini** built by P. F. Silvani and A. Ferri (1648-1656). One of the outstanding examples of Florentine Baroque, the palace consists of a main section flanked by wings, on top of which is a terrace decorated with statuary. At the far end of the courtyard on the left is a great spiral staircase designed by Silvani and on the right a monumental one designed by Ferri and decorated with several antique statues, including one of Clement XII. On the second floor is a fine little art museum, **Galleria Corsini.** The collection, started by Lorenzo Corsini in 1765, is one of the outstanding private collections in Italy. There are works by Raphael, Filippino Lippi, Andrea del Castagno, Botticelli, Signorelli, Caravaggio, Andrea del Sarto, as well as 17th and 18th century Italian and foreign masters. Lungarno Corsini ends at the bridge known as Ponte alla Carraia (rebuilt) at Piazza Goldoni. If we continue along the river the street name changes to Lungarno Amerigo Vespucci which runs into Piazza Ognissanti. Going on even farther, and meanwhile enjoying the lovely view on the other side of the river (the dome of the Cestello Church, with Mount Oliveto in the background, and the San Miniato hill on the left), we soon come to the Amerigo Vespucci bridge.

The bridge was named after the great explorer who discovered Brazil and whose name honors two continents. Built in 1957, the bridge was designed by Enzo Gori, Giuseppe Gori, Ernesto Nelli, and Riccardo Morandi. The *"lungarno"* ends at the reconstructed Ponte della Vittoria on the left and a huge landscaped square to the right. The square, Piazza Vittorio Veneto, has an *equestrian statue of King Vittorio Emanuele II* by Emilio Zocchi (1890). This is the beginning of the **Cascine Park** which extends over 2 miles along the right bank of the Arno. Originally the tree-shaded park was one of the Medici properties with great pastures where cattle could graze (*"cascine"* means dairy-farm). Opened to the public in the middle of the 18th century, it has become one of the city's favorite recreational grounds. There are also public buildings in the Cascine such as the Agricultural Department of the University of Florence, an agricultural institute, the Air Force Academy and sporting centers such as the local racetrack, tennis clubs, sailboat basin, and sporting grounds. At the far end of the park grounds is a monument, dubbed *"l'Indiano"* by the Florentines. It is actually the *tomb of an Indian prince, the Maharajah of Kolopoor,* who died on a trip to Florence in 1870 when he was little more than twenty. He was cremated here, in accordance with the Brahmin custom, at the point where two rivers meet (here the Mugnone flows into the Arno).

Piazza Ognissanti — In the middle is a 19th century sculpture by Romanelli of *Hercules slaying the lion.* Facing into the square is the Baroque façade of the **church of Ognissanti** (All Saints), first built in the 13th century and altered in the Baroque period (1600s). Above the portal is a glazed terracotta of the *Coronation of the Virgin* by Benedetto Buglioni. The lovely belltower dates from the original 13th century complex. The aisleless interior contains some great works of art such as Domenico Ghirlandaio's fresco (second altar on the right) of the *Vespucci family sheltered beneath the Virgin's cloak* (c. 1470). The youth dressed in red between the Virgin and the old man is Amerigo Vespucci himself. Between the third and fourth altars is a fresco of *St. Augustine in his study* by Botticelli. In the chapel of the right transept is a small disk which marks the spot where Botticelli is buried. The frescoes in the dome and four pendentives of the main chapel are by Giovanni da San Giovanni (1617). Opposite Botticelli's fresco of St. Augustine is one of *St. Jerome in his study* by Ghirlandaio (1480). From the left side of church we enter the lovely Renaissance cloister with frescoed lunettes by Giovanni da San Giovanni (1616-1619) and Jacopo Ligozzi (1625). The subject of the frescoes is the life of St. Francis. From the cloister we pass directly into the refectory. On the far wall is Ghirlandaio's renowned *Last Supper* fresco (1480). It is said that Leonardo da Vinci drew his inspiration for his own version of the scene (in the Dominican monastery adjoining the church of Santa Maria delle Grazie in Milan) from Ghirlandaio's masterpiece.

After continuing down Borgo Ognissanti, we turn left into Via dei Fossi which leads right into Piazza Santa Maria Novella.

Piazza Santa Maria Novella — This is one of the most beautiful squares in the city with its lovely 15th century arcade, the **Loggia of San Paolo,** and opposite it, the striking façade of the church of Santa Maria Novella. The loggia is adorned with glazed terracotta medallions by Giovanni della Robbia and a fine lunette with the *Coronation*

Church of Santa Maria Novella.

of St. Dominic by Andrea della Robbia beneath the arcade. The two marble obelisks in the middle of the square are by Giambologna (1608). Surmounted by a bronze fleur-de-lis and resting upon bronze tortoises, these columns once served as boundary markers for a famous chariot race which Cosimo I, inspired by Roman chariot contests, instituted in 1563.

THE CHURCH OF SANTA MARIA NOVELLA — This is the main church of the Dominican order, the counterpart of Santa Croce for the Franciscans. Santa Maria Novella, considered a masterpiece of Italian Gothic architecture, was designed by two monks belonging to the order, Sisto da Firenze and Ristoro da Campi. It was completed in 1360 by another monk, Jacopo Talenti who also designed the graceful Romanesque-Gothic belltower. The Gothic building, with its distinctive green and white striped marble decoration, received its crowning touches between 1456-1470 when Leon Battista Alberti added on the upper section of the façade and the central portal in the Renaissance style. From this unusual combination, a new harmonious blend of styles was born. On either side of the façade and on the external wall of the cloisters are Gothic-style tombs, belonging to famous Florentine families.

113

Santa Maria Novella - Interior.

THE INTERIOR — The interior, shaped like an Egyptian cross, with a single-aisle plan, is a splendid example of the harmonious Italian Gothic style. The altars along the aisles are by Vasari (1565-1571). Right aisle: in the second bay is the *Monument of the Blessed Villana dei Cerchi* by Bernardo Rossellino (1451). Just beyond the fifth bay is the entrance to the **Cappella della Pura** (1474). The *wooden crucifix* on the altar is painted with scenes of the life of Christ (early 14th century). The door on the right leads to the old cemetery with several wall tombs and coats-of-arms. Right transept; on the right is a *tabernacle with a bust of St. Antonino* (15th century). High up is the Gothic *tomb of Tedice Aliotti, Bishop of Fiesole* (d. 1336), by the Sienese sculptor, Tino di Camaino. On the left is the *tomb of Aldobrando Cavalcanti, Bishop of Orvieto* by Nino Pisano. Below it is the *tomb of Joseph, Patriarch of Constantinople* who died in Florence in 1439.

The end of the transept leads up to the **Cappella Rucellai** where Duccio's famous *Virgin enthroned* of c. 1285 (now one of the Uffizi's treasures) originally hung. On the walls are remains of 14th century frescoes depicting the *Martyrdom of St. Catherine.* On the far wall of the transept is the **Cappella Bardi** with remains of frescoes by followers of Giotto (14th century). On the pillar to the right of the entrance is a 13th century relief of *St. George in the act of blessing.* On the right is a two-part window dating from the original 13th century building. Next we come to **Cappella Filippo Strozzi** frescoed by Filippino Lippi (1503) with *Scenes from the lives of the apostles Philip and John*. This is one of the master's last works. The figures on the ceiling are Adam, Noah, Abraham, and Jacob. Behind the altar is the fine carved *tomb of Filippo*

114

Strozzi by Benedetto da Maiano (1491-1493). **Cappella dell'Altar Maggiore:** before the steps is the bronze *tomb slab of Leonardo Dati* by Lorenzo Ghiberti (1423). To the right of the altar is a lovely candleholder shaped like a twisted column, for the candle lit on Easter, by Pier Giovanni Tedesco (14th century). Its companion is a copy. On the modern altar is a bronze *crucifix*, by Giambologna. Apse: the wooden choir fittings and lectern by Baccio d'Agnolo were retouched by Vasari. In the chapel is the renowned fresco cycle on the *life of the Virgin and St. John the Baptist* painted by Ghirlandaio whose helpers included a talented young artist, Michelangelo (1485-1490). The figures are portraits of members of the Tornabuoni family who commissioned the work and friends of theirs, making the frescoes a valuable chronicle of 15th century Florentine life.

On the ceiling are the four Evangelists. The Life of Mary on the left wall starting from below has the following scenes: 1) *Joachim expelled from the Temple as he was childless,* 2) *Birth of the Virgin,* 3) *Presentation of the Virgin at the Temple,* 4) *Marriage of the Virgin,* 5) *Adoration of the Magi,* 6) *Slaughter of the Innocents* and, in the lunette, *Death and Assumption of the Virgin.* Far wall, in the lunette, *Coronation of the Virgin,* on either side of the window, *St. Dominic burning heretical books, Death of St. Peter Martyr,* the *Annunciation, St. John in the desert.* Below, the praying figures are portraits of Francesco Tornabuoni and his wife Francesca Pitti, the donors. On the opposite wall starting from the lower righthand side is the life of the Baptist: *the Angel appearing to Zacharias, the Birth of the Baptist, Zacharias writing his son's name, the Baptist preaching, the Baptism of Christ,* and in the lunette, *Herod's feast.* Left transept: **Cappella Gondi** with remains of 13th century frescoes by Greek artists and a painted wooden *crucifix* by Filippino Brunelleschi. The crucifix has been called "Christ of the eggs" from the time Donatello (who had done a crucifix criticized by Brunelleschi now in the church of Santa Croce) was so struck by its beauty that he dropped the eggs he was holding. Next is the **Cappella Gaddi** with stuccoes and ceiling frescoes by Alessandro Allori. On the altar is a painting of Christ performing a miracle by Bronzino. Passing to the left side of the transept we climb a few steps to the **Cappella Strozzi** with frescoes by Nardo di Cione (c. 1357) depicting the *Last Judgment,* in the middle, *Inferno,* on the right, and *Paradise,* on the left, inspired by Dante's *Divine Comedy.* In the Paradise scene is a portrait of Dante who died in 1321, just a few years before the frescoes were painted. From this side we enter the **sacristy** designed by Jacopo Talenti (1350). Of note are a glazed *terracotta washstand* by Giovanni della Robbia (1498) and two *Crucifixions,* one attributed to Giotto and one to Maso di Bartolomeo. Left aisle: along the wall is one of Masaccio's last and greatest works, a fresco of the *Holy Trinity* (c. 1428) with its unusual perspective view. By the next to last pillar is a *pulpit* designed by Brunelleschi and carved by his follower, Andrea Cavalcanti (1492). To the right of the first altar is the *tomb of A. Strozzi* by Andrea Ferrucci da Fiesole and his helpers (1524).

Cloisters of Santa Maria Novella — The entrance to the cloisters is to the left of the church façade. The first cloister you pass through is the **Chiostro Verde** which is the oldest of the three, having been built in the mid 1300s by a monk, Giovanni da Campi, in the Romanesque style. The cloister's name, *Verde,* comes from the predominant earth green hues of the frescoes painted by Paolo Uccello in the 14th century once decorating them. Now there are only traces of the original series visible (probably by pupils), while two extant frescoes, the *Deluge* and *scenes from the life of Noah,* by Uccello, have been moved to the nearby refectory for safekeeping. Off this cloister is the chapel called **Cappella degli Spagnuoli** (The Spanish Chapel), since Eleanor of Toledo, Cosimo I's wife, had assigned it to the Spanish members of her entourage. Originally the Dominicans' Chapter Room, it was built by Jacopo Talenti in 1359 in honor of St. Thomas of Aquinas and frescoed by a Florentine painter, nevertheless heavily influenced by the Sienese school, Andrea di Bonaiuto, known as Andrea da Firenze (1366-1368). The subjects of the frescoes were given by a Dominican theologian, Fra Zanobi dei Guasconi, then prior of the monastery. On the left wall we see the *Triumph of St. Thomas of Aquinas,* on the right one, the *Militant Church,* on the far wall and ceiling, *scenes from the New Testament,* and on the entrance wall, *stories of St. Peter Martyr.* The cycle is so full of theological symbols and content that it is considered a doctrinal treatise in images. To the left of the *Cappella degli Spagnuoli* a corridor leads to the **Chiostrino dei Morti** which contains numerous tombs and frescoes by followers of Orcagna. In the lunette is a *Noli me tangere* from the della Robbia workshop. Adjoining this cloister is the **Chiostro Grande,** its fifty arches making it one of the largest in Florence. It is decorated with 16th-17th century frescoes, but these are not visible to the public as the cloister is now part of the local police academy.

FIFTH ITINERARY

Piazza del Duomo - Via Cavour - Last Supper in Sant'Apollonia - Cloister dello Scalzo - Piazza San Marco (Church of San Marco; San Marco or Fra Angelico Museum) - Academy Gallery and David statue - Piazza Santissima Annunziata (Church of Santissima Annunziata; Hospital of the Innocents; Archeological Museum) - Synagogue - Cloister of Santa Maria Maddalena de' Pazzi - Church of Sant'Ambrogio.

Via Cavour — This thoroughfare, a continuation of Via Martelli, is always thronged with shoppers and passers-by. On the left corner, where the street starts, is the stately Medici-Riccardi Palace, a thorough description of which appears in the First Itinerary. Farther up the street, on the left side of Piazza San Marco, we turn off into Via degli Arazzieri. A few yards down, Via degli Arazzieri intersects Via XXVII Aprile on which (at number 1) we find the Sant'Apollonia Monastery. Returning to Via Cavour, we reach number 63, now the Court of Appeals. This enormous building complex is on the site of what once was Medici property, which originally consisted of a house set in a magnificent park. It had been purchased in the 15th century by Lorenzo the Magnificent's wife, Clarice Orsini. Lorenzo made it into a meeting-place for the Florentine intelligensia of the day, the literary and artistic greats then under Medici patronage. Lorenzo kept his fabulous art collection of antique statuary, bas-reliefs, and also works by his contemporaries here. Still farther on, at number 69, is the *Chiostro dello Scalzo*.

Cenacolo di Sant'Apollonia (Last Supper by Castagno) — (Entrance at number 1 Via XXVII Aprile, ring for custodian). In this old refectory of the Benedictine monastery of Sant'Apollonia is Andrea Castagno's *Last Supper* fresco, dated 1450-1457. On the left wall we see the *Crucifixion, Deposition,* and *Resurrection* and in the two lunettes, a *Crucifixion* and a *Pietà*.

Chiostro dello Scalzo — (Via Cavour 69, ring for the custodian). The cloister is called *"dello Scalzo"* (of the barefoot man) because the crossbearer of this religious confraternity (founded in 1376) used to walk barefoot in religious processions. The early 16th century cloister is known for the *chiaroscuro frescoes* that Andrea del Sarto masterfully painted on the walls between 1514 and 1526. Two of the sixteen scenes from the life of *St. John the Baptist,* however, are by Franciabigio.

Piazza San Marco — In the middle of the landscaped island is a *monument to General Manfredo Fanti,* by Pio Fedi (1837). The buildings on the square include the church of San Marco and its adjacent monastery (which is also the Fra Angelico Museum), the headquarters of the University of Florence, and the corner of Via Ricasoli, the **Academy of Beaux Arts** (you can see its 14th century porch), once part of the Hospital of San Matteo.
The Academy Museum (where Michelangelo's original David may be viewed) is at Via Ricasoli 52.

THE CHURCH OF SAN MARCO — Althought it originally went up at the end of the 13th century in Romanesque-Gothic style, it was rebuilt when Cosimo the Elder commissioned Michelozzo to remodel it for the Dominican friars in 1452.
Remodeled once more by Giambologna in 1580, it was not until 1678 that Pier Francesco Silvani, making even greater changes, gave it its present appearance. The Baroque façade was designed

Piazza San Marco.

by a monk, Fra Gioacchino Pronti, in 1780, although the wooden portal was already in place during the lifetime of the famous Dominican monk, Savonarola (1490s). In fact, we know it withstood an attempt made to set it on fire when a revolt broke out — enraged citizens were trying to get into the church so they could capture and kill Savonarola.

THE INTERIOR — The painting on the lovely carved ceiling of the aisleless church depicts the *Virgin in Glory* (by G. Antonio Pucci, 1725). Over the entranceway is a huge *crucifix* by followers of Giotto (17th century). At the first altar on the righthand side is *St. Thomas of Aquinas* by Santi di Tito, at the second *Virgin and saints* by Fra Bartolomeo (1509), at the third a huge 8th century mosaic of the *Virgin in prayer* (it originally belonged to Pope John VII's oratory), and, at the fourth, framed by an *arch surmounted by a statue of St. Zenobius* by Giambologna (1580), the *Virgin with an image of St. Dominic* by Matteo Rosselli. At the end of the nave a Baroque door leads to the vestibule and sacristy designed by Michelozzo (1437-1443), inside of which is a *reclining statue of St. Antonino* designed by Giambologna and executed by Portinari. To the left of the *Cappella Maggiore* is another chapel, the *Cappella Serragli* or *Sacramento* decorated with frescoes by Santi di Tito and Passignano. Next comes the *Cappella Salviati* or Sant'Antonino Chapel, designed by Giambologna and built during the years 1580-1589. The subject of the fine frescoes by Passignano is the *Burial of St. Antonino.* The bronze and marble decoration is also by Giambologna and Pietro Francavilla, one of his pupils. The wall tombs of two of the best-known humanists, *Pico della Mirandola* and *Poliziano,* are along the left wall of the church.

117

San Marco Museum - Sant'Antonino Cloister.

THE SAN MARCO OR FRA ANGELICO MUSEUM — The entrance to the museum is just to the right of the church. The museum was originally a monastery, first belonging to the Vallombrosan and later to the Silvestrini orders. In the 1430s Cosimo the Elder commissioned Michelozzo to redo the whole building. By the time Michelozzo started work on the project (1437-1457), the monastery had been turned over to the Dominicans, the order of Fra Angelico. The painter–friar lived here between 1435 to 1445. Other famous men as well lived in San Marco: Girolamo Savonarola (1489-1498), Sant'Antonino Pierozzi, Archbishop of Florence, and Fra Bartolomeo, another great Renaissance painter-friar. When the monastery was surpressed in 1866, it was turned into a state museum, mainly for the Fra Angelico paintings formerly scattered amongst Florentine museums and churches.

San Marco Museum - Flight into Egypt by Fra Angelico (detail).

The cloister of Sant'Antonino – A typical example of Renaissance monastic architecture, the cloister is decorated with 16th-17th century frescoes of scenes from the life of St. Antonino. Of particular note is the lunette fresco (near the *Ospizio* entrance) by Bernardino Poccetti showing the original façade of the Cathedral of Florence designed by Arnolfo di Cambio. Several frescoes by Fra Angelico are to be found here: *St. Peter the Martyr* (far end, left, in the lunette over the door), *St. Dominic at the foot of the Cross* (on the wall opposite the entrance) *Pietà* (at the end of the same wall, above the door) and *Christ clad as a pilgrim received by the Dominican monks* (over the doorway of the next wall).

Ospizio dei Pellegrini (Pilgrims' Lodgings) – This is the world's foremost collection of paintings by the mystic monk and artist, Fra Angelico, who reputedly could not paint a Crucifixion without weeping. It is divided into three sections. In the first section is the renowned *Linaioli Altarpiece* which depicts the Virgin enthroned and music-

119

making angels (1433); the lovely marble frame was designed by Ghiberti. In addition, there are several other noteworthy panels such as the *Marriage* and *Death of the Virgin, Zacharias writing his son's name,* two versions of the *Virgin enthroned,* and the *Miracle and burial of Sts. Cosmas and Damian.* The second section contains thirty-five panels with *scenes from the life of Christ* (1450). They originally made up the wings of the Crucifixion Altarpiece in the church of Santissima Annunziata. The *Flight into Egypt, Nativity,* and *Christ entering Jerusalem* panels are by Angelico's own hand, whereas the rest were done with the help of other artists except for three by Alessio Baldovinetti. The outstanding works in the third section include the *Virgin of the Star,* the *Last Judgment,* the *Coronation of the Virgin,* the *Deposition,* the *Annunciation,* and the *Adoration of the Magi.*

Sala del Lavabo (The Font Room) — The baptismal font is from the della Robbia workshop. Among the 16th century paintings decorating the walls is an interesting chiaroscuro *Virgin and saints* by Fra Bartolomeo.

The Main Refectory — The room is hung with works by Fra Bartolomeo, including his fine *Last Judgment.* The huge fresco showing *St. Dominic's miraculous supper* was painted by Giovanni Antonio Sogliani (1536).

The Chapter Room — Here the monks, after having confessed their sins, awaited the punishment meted out by their superior—the painting of *St. Thomas of Aquinas with the Book of Discipline* in the lunette over the doorway is a symbolic representation of this. Opposite the entrance is a Fra Angelico painting of the *Crucifixion with various saints and the founders of the religious orders,* a superb blend of dramatic effect and refined pictorial style. On the left wall is a tempera on canvas of *St. Antonino in adoration* by Baldovinetti (16th century) and opposite, a painted wood *crucifix* by Baccio da Montelupo (1500).

Second floor — At the top of the stairs are frescoes of the *Annunciation* and *St. Dominic adoring the Cross,* two marvelous examples of Fra Angelico's mysticism translated into imagery. On either side of the hallways are little cubicles, once the cells inhabited by the Dominican monks. Each one contains a fresco, either by Fra Angelico himself or by his pupils who worked from his designs. The outstanding frescoes are: *Noli me tangere* (cell 1), the *Annunciation* (cell 3), the *Crucifixion* (cell 4), the *Transfiguration* (cell 6), the *Mocking of Christ* (cell 7), the *Coronation of the Virgin* (cell 9), and the *Virgin and Child with saints* (cell 11).

At the end of the corridor we come to the **Quartiere del Priore** (Prior's Apartments). Here, in this three-room apartment, Fra Girolamo Savonarola, the reformer monk, made his home until April 8, 1498 when he was taken off to be tried for heresy. In the first cell, the vestibule, are two paintings of Savonarola being burned at the stake on May 3, 1498, by painters of the period. There are also two *portraits* by Fra Bartolomeo, one of *Savonarola* and one of *St. Peter Martyr.* In the second cell (study) is a wooden *crucifix* by Baccio da Montelupo that belonged to Savonarola. The bibles on the desk as well as the chalices, cowl, tunic, and crown in the cabinet all once belonged to the monk. In the third cell (bedroom) is a processional standard with a *Crucifixion* painted in the style of Fra Angelico. Retracing our steps, we can stop at the cells along the left side frescoed with crucifixions by pupils of Fra Angelico. In cell 31, once inhabited by St. Antonino we can see manuscripts handwritten by the saint himself, several reliquaries, and the saint's deathmask. The frescoes in the entrance and cells 34 (*Sermon in the garden*) and 35 (*Communion of the Apostles*) by Fra Angelico's helpers, are particularly worthy of note. At the end of the righthand corridor are two cells, 38 and 39, which were used by Cosimo the Elder for spiritual retreats. In the first cell is a *Crucifixion* by Fra Angelico, who was aided by Benozzo Gozzoli. In the second are a *bust of St. Antonino* and a *portrait of Cosimo* attributed to Pontormo.

The Library — This lovely Renaissance hall with its graceful Ionic columns was designed by Michelozzo (1441). The showcases contain precious 14th-15th century manuscripts, many of which illuminated.

The Refectory — Returning to the ground floor we enter the refectory decorated with a fresco of the *Last Supper* by Ghirlandaio. It greatly resembles the fresco of the same subject he painted in the refectory of Ognissanti.

The Cloister of San Domenico — It too was designed by Michelozzo. Along the arcades and in the adjoining rooms are fragments from the medieval buildings in the old center of Florence torn down in the 19th century.

San Marco Museum - *Above:* Annunciation by Fra Angelico;
below: Virgin and Child with Saints by Fra Angelico.

Academy Gallery - Tribune with Michelangelo's David.

THE ACADEMY GALLERY — This museum came into being when Pietro Leopoldo I, the Lorraine grandduke, set up a collection of great masters so that young art students enrolled in the Beaux Arts Academy could study them. As time went on, the collection was enriched by works removed from suppressed monasteries and churches. The collection has undergone changes and rearrangements as new concepts of museum layout have been introduced in the city's museums.

The present collection entails minor works of great masters from the 1200s to 1500s. But the gallery's claim to fame is its collection of sculpture masterpieces by Michelangelo. Perhaps the most famous of all is the David. The statue, which once stood before Palazzo Vecchio in Piazza della Signoria, was placed in the so-called *"Tribuna"* especially designed for it by the architect De Fabris. Removed from the open air square for safekeeping, it was set up here in 1882.

Academy Gallery - Two Slaves by Michelangelo; *right:*
Palestrina "Pietà" by Michelangelo.

ROOM I — The entrance is right off the vestibule where the ticket counter has been
set up. The works displayed are 16th century paintings, including several by Francesco
Granacci, the *Annunciation* and other paintings by Mariotto Albertinelli, *St. John the
Baptist* and *Mary Magdalen* by Filippino Lippi, a fine *Deposition* by Lippi and Perugino,
a *Virgin and saints* by Perugino, a *Virgin and Child with saints* by Ghirlandaio, as well
as others by Fra Bartolomeo and Francesco Botticini. The sculpture in the middle
is Giambologna's *Rape of the Sabine Women*.

THE HALL AND THE "TRIBUNE" — From room 1 we enter the main hall. You don't have to be an art expert to realize that we are in the presence of genius, the unmistakable greatness of Michelangelo. This is evident even in the uncompleted *Slaves* seemingly struggling to free themselves from the stone they are bound in. These, plus the Slaves in the Louvre, were begun by Michelangelo in 1518 for Pope Julius II's tomb, but none of them was ever finished. Farther on is another unfinished masterpiece, the *St. Matthew* of 1518. This is the only one of the 12 apostles originally planned for the Cathedral of Florence ever begun. Oddly enough, it is this unifnished look which lends a particularly modern touch to their intrinsic beauty. Michelangelo's conception of art is to attack the marble block so that he can free living forms bound in the inert stone. Perhaps his creative urge was satisfied by this act of liberation, and thus he needed to go no further than the early stages. In fact, before the Slaves, we are struck by how little they have to do with matter, but rather how hard they are vainly struggling to escape from their enforced immobility.

Behind the statues are Flemish and Florentine *tapestries* dating from the 16th through 18th centuries with scenes from Genesis. Beyond the St. Matthew is one of Michelangelo's famous *Pietàs*, the *Pietà of Palestrina* carved by the artist when he was an old man for the chapel of Palazzo Barberini in Palestrina. Despite the fact that for years art historians have been arguing over the attribution to Michelangelo, our feeling is that only Michelangelo, could convey such a sense of sorrow and death without having to go beyond the *"non-finito"* look. Dominating the Tribune is the celebrated statue of David moved here from Piazza della Signoria (a copy has been put up in its place). Commissioned of 26-year-old Michelangelo by the Republic of Florence as a symbol of liberty to stand before the town hall, Palazzo Vecchio, the giant figure was sculpted in just four years (1501-1504). The youthful David exudes strength and virility, a fitting symbol of freedom for the proud Florentines. Nevertheless, Michelangelo's youth is telling — the figure is not perfect, anatomically speaking that is. In fact, a close look reveals that, while the figure's hips are rather slight for such a well-developed torso, his head, hands, and feet are overly large in proportion to the rest of the body. But the overall effect is of great beauty and we can easily dismiss such minor defects before the grandeur of the whole.

ROOM V — Off the David Tribune is the museum's collection of 13th century Tuscan school paintings. One of the most interesting is a large panel painting with *Mary Magdalen*. It is by an unknown artist known as the Magdalen Master from this painting (two other works by this painter are also on display here). In addition, there are a huge wooden *crucifix* of the 13th century Sienese school, a huge *Tree of the Cross*, and a *Crucifixion* altarpiece by Pacino di Buonaguida.

ROOM VI — This room features 14th century Florentine school paintings, including a fine altarpiece with the *Coronation of the Virgin* by Bernardo Daddi, a painting of the same subject by Jacopo di Cione, a huge 14th century wood *crucifix*, and Orcagna's *Virgin and Child Altarpiece*.

ROOM VII — There are several interesting works here, including a wooden *crucifix*, school of Bernardo Daddi, a fine *Pietà* by Giovanni da Milano, and a *Virgin and Child* by Taddeo Gaddi. There are also works by the Master of the Rinuccini Chapel, as well as the *Lives of Christ and St. Francis* cycle, originally part of the reliquary cabinet in the sacristy of Santa Croce.

ROOM II — Crossing the Hall of the Slaves we reach Room 2, which features Early Renaissance Florentine art. There are some excellent paintings (a *Virgin and Child* by Mariotto di Cristofano, an *Annunciation* by Filippino Lippi, and a *Trinity* by Domenico di Michelino), but perhaps the most interesting piece is a hopechest, the *Cassone Adimari*, decorated with a charming scene of a wedding procession in 15th century Florence.

ROOM III — The outstanding paintings displayed here are Perugino's *Visitation*, Botticelli's *Virgin and Child*, and a *Thebaid* attributed to Paolo Uccello.

ROOM IV — On the stand is a charming Virgin and Child known as the *Madonna del Mare* by Botticelli, and by the same painter, the *Virgin enthroned* hung nearby. An *Adoration with angels* by Lorenzo di Credi, a *Pietà* by Jacopo del Sellaio, a *Resurrection* by Raffaellino del Garbo, plus other works by Bartolomeo di Giovanni, Cosimo Rosselli, and Botticini are also displayed.

Going back to Piazza San Marco, we make a right turn into Via Cesare Battisti which leads into Piazza Santissima Annunziata.

Academy Gallery - Madonna del Mare by Botticelli.

Piazza Santissima Annunziata - In the background is the porch leading to the church entrance. On the right you can see the archways of Brunelleschi's Spedale degli Innocenti. In the middle is the equestrian monument to Grandduke Ferdinand I.

Piazza Santissima Annunziata — This square, of perfect proportions and dimensions which enhance rather than dwarf man, embodies the true essence of the Renaissance spirit. Bounded on three sides by lovely arcading, the square is decorated with an *equestrian statue of Grandduke Ferdinando I,* a late work designed by Giambologna and executed by Pietro Tacca (1608), and two elegant Baroque *fountains with bronze sea monsters,* by Tacca and helpers (1629). To the right of the church of Santissima Annunziata is Brunelleschi's *Spedale degli Innocenti* (Foundling Hospital), while on the left is the **Confraternita dei Servi di Maria,** by Antonio da Sangallo the Elder and Baccio d'Agnolo (1516-1525), whose arcade repeats the elegant lines of Brunelleschi's across the square.

Spedale degli Innocenti — A jewel of Early Renaissance architecture, the building was designed by Brunelleschi who worked on it from 1421 to 1424, although it was completed by Francesco della Luna in 1445. The ten glazed ceramic *medallions with babes in swaddling clothes* by Andrea della Robbia (1463) are fitting decoration to the marvelous arcade. Beneath the loggia are frescoes by Poccetti. In the lunette over the lefthand portal is a fresco of *God the Father with martyr saints* by Giovanni di Francesco (1458). — Inside the hospital, a charitable organization founded by the Florentine Republic in 1421 as a home for orphans and unwanted illegitimate infants, we first encounter a lovely arcaded courtyard which is decorated with another glazed terracotta by Andrea della Robbia, this one of the *Annunciation* (in the lefthand lunette). The corridor on the right leads us to the **Art Gallery** which features a number of noteworthy works despite its small size (5 rooms). The collection includes the *Adoration of the Magi* Ghirlandaio painted especially for the hospital and a *Virgin and Child with angels* by Botticelli, as well as paintings by Pietro di Cosimo, Giovanni del Biondo, Neri di Bicci, sculpture by Luca della Robbia (do not overlook the exquisite *Virgin*), and portraits of the Spedale's benefactors.

128

THE CHURCH OF SANTISSIMA ANNUNZIATA — Inside this church is the much venerated holy image of the Virgin known as the *"Madonna Annunziata"* (the Virgin Annunciate). Originally built around 1250 by the seven monks who founded the order of the Servants of Mary, the church was remodeled by Michelozzo in 1444 and then again in the 17th and 18th centuries. The seven-arch porch leading to the church proper was built in 1601 by Giovanni Caccini. The central arch, with a fresco by Pontormo portraying Charity and Faith, is earlier than the others and has been attributed to Antonio da Sangallo the Elder. Above the central portal is a fine mosaic of an Annunciation scene done by Davide Ghirlandaio in 1509.

The arcade leads to an atrium known as the **Chiostrino dei Voti** built by Antonio Manetti in 1447 after Michelozzo's design. The subjects of the interesting frescoes in the lunettes are (starting from the one to the right of the entrance): the *Assumption* by Giovanni Battista Rosso (1517) the *Visitation* by Pontormo (1516) the *Marriage of the Virgin* by Franciabigio (1513), a relief carving of the *Virgin* by Michelozzo, the *Birth of the Virgin,* one of Andrea del Sarto's best-known works (1514), the *Three Magi,* also by del Sarto (1513), a *Christmas scene* by Alessio Baldovinetti (1462, and thus the oldest fresco here), the *Vocation of St. Filippo Benizzi* by Cosimo Rosselli (1476), and others with *episodes from the life of St. Filippo* by Andrea del Sarto. There is a *bust of Andrea del Sarto* by Caccini on the wall.

THE INTERIOR — The interior reflects the Baroque taste for elaborate decoration. Aisleless, it has deep lateral chapels and a carved ceiling adorned with stuccowork. To the left of the entrance is a marble temple designed by Michelozzo (1448) and put up by Lapo Portigiani. It protects an elaborate altar which contains a miraculous image of the Virgin (generally veiled). According to legend, the image — a 14th century Florentine school panel of no particular merit — was actually painted by a certain Bartolomeo who fell asleep over his work only to find that an angel had painted in the Virgin's head in the meantime. The hanging lamps, candlesticks, silver altar and altarfront were donated by the Medici granddukes. — In the first chapel on the left, *St. Julian*, remains of a fresco by Andrea del Castagno. In the second chapel, the *Trinity, the three Marys, and St. Jerome* by Andrea del Castagno. In the fourth chapel, the *Assumption of the Virgin* by Perugino and helpers. In the *Cappella del Crocifisso* in the left transept is a terracotta statue of *St. John the Baptist* by Michelozzo. The corridor on the right leads to the sacristy designed by Michelozzo and built by Lapo Portigiani. In the rotunda: the fresco in the dome of the *Coronation of the Virgin* is by Volterrano. On the left is the *tomb of Bishop Angelo Marzi Medici* by Francesco da Sangallo (1546). On the floor is the *tomb slab of Andrea del Sarto*. Behind the choir, the center chapel, the *Cappella del Soccorso*, was designed by Giambologna as a burial place for himself and the other Flemish artists who died in Florence. The *crucifix* on the altar and the bronze bas-reliefs depicting *scenes of the Passion* are also by Giambologna. The chapel on the left contains a *Resurrection* by Bronzino and a wooden *statue of St. Roch* by Norimberga Viet Stoss. To the right of the rotunda is the *tomb of Donato dell'Antella* by G. B. Foggini. In the fifth chapel on the right, a *monument to Orlando dei Medici* by Bernardo Rossellino (1456). In the fourth chapel, a marble *Pietà* by Baccio Bandinelli who is buried here (1559). From the left transept, by way of the door opposite the sacristy, we enter the **Chiostro dei Morti** (Cloister of the Dead). Above the north door is a famous fresco by Andrea del Sarto, the *Madonna del Sacco*. The cloister walls are covered with frescoes showing scenes relating to the Order of the Servants of Mary, many of which were painted by Bernardo Focetti. Beneath the portico is the entrance to the **Chapel of St. Luke,** since 1562 headquarters of the "*Compagnia degli Artisti Fiorentini*" (the artists' guild). Among the famous artists buried here are Benvenuto Cellini, Franciabigio, and Pontormo.

THE ARCHEOLOGICAL MUSEUM — The museum, actually the Crocetta Palace, has one of the finest collections of archeological pieces to be found in Italy. The three major divisions are Etruscan topography, the Egyptian museum, and the Etruscan-Greek-Roman Antiquarium.

On the ground floor are two recently arranged rooms. The first features the renowned *François vase* displayed in the center of the room. This masterpiece of 6th century B.C. Attic figure painting, decorated with mythological scenes, is signed by the potter Ergotimos and painter Kleitias. The photos and explanatory notes posted on the walls document the painstaking steps in the restoration of the vase. In the second room are four Etruscan funerary urns from Chiusi and Chianciano, one of which is the famous *Mater Matuta*. Photos and explanatory text provide valuable information on the exhibit.

On the second floor are the Etrusco-Roman and Egyptian collections.

The Egyptian Museum — The collection, second only to the Turin collection, was founded in 1824. It is composed of the finds excavated under the supervision of Ippolito Rossellini, as well as pieces donated from private collections. The eight-room museum has a vast collection of sarcophagi, mummies, sculpture, jewelry, papyri, etc. of different periods. The highlights are: a fragment from a granite sculpture with the Goddess Hathor as a cow nuturing the Pharoah Harembed (14th century B.C.), a bust of a pharoah in red basalt (13th century B.C.), a painted relief of the Goddess Hathor holding out her hand to the Pharoah Sethos (13th century B.C.), two statuettes of young girls making beer and a third making flour (1625-2475 B.C.), and a wood and bone chariot found in a necropolis at Thebes (14th century B.C.).

The Etruscan-Greek-Roman Antiquarium — The collection is made up of pieces originally part of the Medicis' and Lorraine granddukes' private collections, further enriched by bequests and purchases. It consists mainly of sculptures and bronzes. The most important exhibits are: the *sarcophagus of Ramta Uznai* (1st century B.C.), *Minerva from Arezzo* (school of Praxiteles), *Chimera from Arezzo* Etruscan, 5th

Archeological Museum - Haranger.

century B.C.), the *Haranger* (statue honoring a prominent Etruscan, Aulus Metellus, dating around the 3rd-2nd century B.C.), the *Idolino* (Greek original of the 5th century B.C.), *Horse's head* (this Hellenistic work inspired the horse of Donatello's famous Gattamelata equestrian monument which the great artist erected in Padua). — On the same floor are the Coin and Jewel Collection (gemstones, cameos, silver, etc.). On the third floor are the Etruscan-Greek-Roman collections. The works exhibited come from both north and south Italy, Cyprus, Crete, Greece, and Rhodes, including an extensive collection of 6th century B.C. Attic and black figure vases, Etruscan ceramics, frescoes detached from Etruscan tombs, reproductions of Etruscan painting from Vulci, Tarquinia, and Chiusi tombs, and a painted sarcophagus of Larthis Seiantus (3rd-2nd century B.C.).

Via della Colonna follows the whole length of the Archeological Museum. On the right side of the street, where it intersects Via della Pergola, is Benvenuto Cellini's house. Here the great jeweler-sculptor modeled and cast the famous Perseus still standing under the Loggia in Piazza Signoria. Further on, at Via della Colonna 7, is the Monastery of Santa Maria Maddalena dei Pazzi which vaunts a famous fresco of a *Crucifixion* by Perugino. The street leads into a pleasantly landscaped square, Piazza d'Azeglio. Turning right into Via Farini we soon come to the **Synagogue** of Florence at number 6. Funded by David Levi's donation to the Jewish University,

Synagogue.

it was designed by a team of architects (Mariano Falcini, Marco Treves, and Vincenzo Micheli) and built between 1872 and 1874. The distinctive Moorish style building is surmounted by a lovely copper dome and decorated with striking stained glass windows. Via Farini leads into Via dei Pilastri where we turn left and shortly reach the church of Sant'Ambrogio in the square of the same name.

Monastery of Santa Maria Maddalena de' Pazzi — (Via della Colonna 7; if it is closed, ring for the custodian). In the Chapter Room of this old monastery is Perugino's famous fresco depicting the *Crucifixion*. The harmonious composition, divided by the arches into three parts, is enhanced by the superb background landscape. In the center is the Crucifixion scene with St. Mary Magdalen in adoration flanked by the Virgin and St. Bernard on the left and Sts. John and Benedict on the right.

The Church of Sant'Ambrogio — Although the original structure dates from 1296, it has since been remodeled. Inside the aisleless church are several superb Renaissance altars and 14th-15th century paintings. The *Cappella del Miracolo* to the left of the choir has a fine tabernacle by Mino da Fiesole (1481), a fresco with a *Procession* by Cosimo Rosselli (1486), and, on the next wall, a painting of *Angels and saints* by Alessio Baldovinetti. On the floor is a plaque indicating the spot where Mino da Fiesole is buried. Among the other famous artists buried here are Andrea del Verrocchio, Simone del Pollaiuolo (Cronaca), and Francesco Granacci.

SIXTH ITINERARY

Piazza del Duomo - Via del Proconsolo - Dante's House - Piazza San Firenze - Bargello Palace (National Museum) - Badia Church - Michelangelo's House - Piazza Santa Croce (Church of Santa Croce; Pazzi Chapel; Santa Croce Museum) - Horne Museum - Bardini Museum.

Via del Proconsolo — This street, which starts at the north side of the Cathedral apse, is one of the oldest in the city (it dates from Roman times). A few yards down is a tiny square, Piazza Santa Maria del Campo, with the church of the same name. Number 12, at the intersection of Borgo degli Albizi, is the so-called **Palazzo Non-finito** (Unfinished Palace). Begun by Bernardo Buontalenti in 1593 (he was commissioned by Alessandro Strozzi), the project was taken up by G. B. Caccini, then continued by Matteo Nigetti, and still others, yet was never completed by anybody. Today it is the **Museum of Anthropology and Ethnology** founded by Paolo Mantegazza and featuring collections relating to African, Asian, Indonesian, Oceanic, and American civilizations. — Across the street, at number 10, is a superb example of the Renaissance palace, **Palazzo Pazzi-Quaratesi,** designed by Giuliano da Maiano for the Pazzi family. — Farther on, we turn right into Via Dante Alighieri which has a picturesque cluster of old buildings midway along it. On the corner is a much-restored building known as the **House of Dante,** supposedly where Dante was born. — Continuing along Via del Proconsolo we see the church of the Badia on the right and across the street, the Palazzo del Bargello, now the National Museum. A few yards further down is Piazza San Firenze.

Piazza San Firenze — With our backs to the 16th century side of Palazzo Vecchio, we get a splendid view of the Bargello with its plain fortress-like façade and sturdy 13th century tower. Opposite it, the slender belltower of the Badia rises out of a cluster of lower buildings, while in the background we see the unmistakable shape of Brunelleschi's dome. On the west side of the square is **Palazzo Gondi,** one of the finest examples of Italian Renaissance architecture.
Designed by Giuliano da Sangallo in 1494, the building also contains a noteworthy courtyard. Opposite is a Baroque complex comprising a central core flanked by a church on either side. Formerly a Filapine monastery, the building is today the Courthouse of Florence whereas the church on the left is still consecrated to St. Firenze.

THE BARGELLO PALACE — The name of the palace dates back to the 15th century when the Captain of Justice otherwise known as "*il Bargello*" established his headquarters in the building. Work on this impressive structure got underway in 1254. Once seat of the Capitan of the People and later that of the *Podestà* (governor), it is the second most important civic building in the city (after Palazzo Vecchio). It has a typically medieval appearance, with little of the Renaissance airiness and lightness. Its distinctive tower has always been known as "*la Volognana.*"

The front (tower side) is the oldest part and was designed by Fra Sisto and Fra Ristoro, the monks who designed the church of Santa Maria Novella. The back was built between 1260 and 1346 by Neri di Fioravante and Benci di Cione who also designed the great hall known as the *Salone del Consiglio* and the courtyard. When the building became the headquarters for the Captain of Justice and the judges of the *Rota* (a kind of civil court), it was turned into a prison and place of execution. The Weapons Room was the torture chamber and the gallows were set up in the courtyard until 1782 when both torture instruments and gallows were burned by order of Grandduke Leopoldo.

The Bargello.

THE NATIONAL MUSEUM – The National Museum has occupied the Bargello Palace since 1859. The collection is of prime importance for an understanding of Tuscan sculpture and minor arts ranging from the 14th to the 16th centuries.

GROUND FLOOR – **The Courtyard**. We step into the courtyard after leaving the vestibule where tickets are sold.
Beneath the arcade are several 16th century Florentine statues. Particulary noteworthy are a number of allegorical figure sulpted by Bartolomeo Ammannati and a reconstruction of a fountain which was supposed to have been built in Palazzo Vecchio, by the same

artist. Other fine works include a statue of *Fiesole* by Tribolo and the *Fisherboy* by the 19th century sculptor, Vincenzo Gemito. The imposing staircase, designed by Neri di Fioravante, beautifully completes the architectural setting. All over the walls and beneath the arcades are the coats-of-arms of *Podestà* (governor) and magistrates, as well as the painted emblems of the various sections of the city.

The Sala del Trecento (14th century sculpture) — This room is opposite the museum entrance. In the middle of the room is a marble holy water font support (school of Nicola Pisano, 13th century). Along the right wall: a marble *Virgin and Child* by the Sienese sculptor Tino di Camaino (14th century), and an alabaster *Virgin and Child* (15th century Venetian school). On the far side: a grandiose *Virgin with Sts, Peter and Paul,* by Paolo di Mastro Giovanni.

The Salone del Cinquecento (Renaissance Sculpture Hall) — Below the courtyard stairs is a hall with massive pillars along it which is a veritable treasurehouse of 16th century sculpture. Of course, there are several Michelangelos: the *Apollo-David,* the powerful bust of *Brutus;* the tipsy *Bacchus,* a youthful work, and the *Virgin and Child* known as the *Pitti Tondo,* which is the sculptural counterpart of the *Doni Tondo* painting in the Uffizi. Benvenuto Cellini is represented by *Apollo and Hyacinth,* the tiny *Perseus, Narcissus,* and others. Other highlights include Jacopo Sansovino's *Bacchus,* the allegorical group of *Florence defeating Pisa* and other statues by Giambologna, as well as the statues Bartolommeo Ammannati carved for the *Nari tomb,* and his interesting version of *Leda and the swan.*

Bargello - Courtyard.

National Museum - Pitti Tondo by Michelangelo.

THE SECOND FLOOR — On a pillar by the staircase is the *seated lion* known as the *Marzocco*, the symbol of Republican Florence. Upstairs on the loggia (**verone**) is a collection of Giambologna's extraordinary sculptures, including his realistic *animal figures* and his world famous bronze *Mercury*.

The Main Hall — This striking room is actually the *Salone del Consiglio Grande* (the General Council Hall). It contains some of the most famous Early Renaissance sculptures to have come out of 15th century Florence, especially the revolutionary creations of Donatello, the foremost *Quattrocento* sculptor. Just as Masaccio brought new ideas to painting, Donatello initiated the new course of sculpture. His free-standing figures, including the bronze David, the first nude since antiquity, are anatomically accurate and naturalistically posed, unlike the stiffer, hieratic Gothic and Romanesque statues that preceded them. His *"stiacciato"* reliefs (a relief consisting of shallowly incised lines) convey the effect of paintings and his use of perspective in them even precedes Masaccio. This can be seen in the *St. George* (removed from Orsanmichele) with the *stiacciato relief of St. George slaying the dragon* on the bottom of the huge tabernacle (1416). Flanking the niche are two busts, one of *Giovanni Antonio da Nanni* and the other, in painted terracotta, of *Niccolò da Uzzano,* plus a relief of the *Crucifixion*. We can also admire an early marble *David* and the famous bronze *David* of 1430, as well as two versions of *St. John the Baptist,* one of which is an early work, while the other is a late one. The works by the other sculptors here, especially those by Desiderio da Settignano (e.g. *bust of St. John*) all reveal Donatello's enormous influence on 15th century sculpture. In addition, you can see and judge for yourself the famous reliefs showing the *Sacrifice of Isaac* that Ghiberti and Bru-

National Museum - *Left:* **Donatello's David;** *right:* **Donatello's St. George.**

nelleschi prepared in 1402 for the competition of the Baptistry door (and which Ghiberti won). Other highlights include a painted plaster relief of the *Virgin and Child with angels* by Agostino di Duccio, two glazed terracottas of the *Virgin* by Luca della Robbia, a bronze relief of a *Battle scene* by Bertoldo, as well as two painted 15th century *chests*.

The Sala della Torre (Tower Room) — In addition to embroidered fabrics and tapestries, there are two superb 14th century French altarpieces.

The Sala del Podestà (Governor's Room) — These enamels, crystalware, and 16th century Venetian, French, and Oriental art treasures originally belonged to the French art collector, M. Louis Carrand, who donated them to the city of Florence in 1888. Of particular note are the Limoges enamels from the 11th to 14th centuries displayed in the first and last showcases.

National Museum - Virgin and Child by Luca della Robbia.

The Cappella del Podestà — Here in this chapel people sentenced to death spent their last few hours in prayer. The frescoes on the walls, sometimes attributed to Giotto, show *Inferno* (by the entrance), *scenes from the life of St. Mary Magdalen, St. Mary of Egypt, and St. John the Baptist (along the sides) and Paradise* (far wall), where you note a (much-repainted) portrait of Dante. The inlaid wooden choir stalls and lectern were carved by Bernardo della Cecca at the end of the 15th century for the church of San Miniato.

The Sala degli Avori (Collection of Ivories) — This is one of the world's finest collection of medieval ivories. In the room are also fine pieces of 14th and 15th century Tuscan wood sculpture.

The Sala delle Oreficerie Sacre (Religious Objects Collection) — The collection of 15th century gold and silver ecclesiastical ornaments includes chalices, processional crosses, and reliquaries of extraordinary workmanship, which originally belonged to Florentine churches. The *reliquary bust of St, Ignatius* is a fine example of 15th century Florentine craftsmanship.

The Sala delle Maioliche — This collection features pieces from the famous pottery works of Faenza, Pesaro, Urbino, and Florence, as well as interesting 16th century Moorish style ceramics from the factory of Valencia.

138

THIRD FLOOR — **The Sala di Giovanni della Robbia.** Among the fine pieces displayed here, two by Giovanni della Robbia, the *Pietà* and the *Noli me tangere,* are particularly outstanding. In addition, there is a bust of *Costanza Bonarelli* by Bernini, the Roman Baroque master, and the *Ganymede,* an antique statue restored by Benvenuto Cellini.

The Sala delle Armature (Weapons Room) — The weapons dating from various periods displayed here mostly belonged to the Medici collections.

The Sala dei della Robbia — These glazed terracottas are by Andrea, Luca, and Giovanni della Robbia and Santi Buglioni.

The Sala del Verrocchio — This room features sculpture by the Florentine artist Andrea de' Cione called Verrocchio (b. 1435-d. 1488) to whom Leonardo da Vinci was apprenticed. The sculptures include the charming bronze *David,* a *bust of a lady with a bouquet of flowers* revealing fine technique and great expressiveness, two versions of the *Virgin* one in terracotta and one in marble, a *bust of Piero di Lorenzo dei Medici,* and a relief of the *Death of Francesca Pitti Tornabuoni.* There are also fine sculptures by Antonio Rossellino, Mino da Fiesole, Benedetto da Maiano, Antonio del Pollaiuolo, Francesco Laurana, and Matteo Cividali.

The Sala del Camino (Fireplace Room) — The room is named after the 16th century carved fireplace from Palazzo Borgherini by Benedetto da Rovezzano. Other Renaissance sculptors represented are Ghiberti, Antonio del Pollaiuolo, Tacca, and M. Soldani. Giambologna's *Labors of Hercules* and the preparatory piece for his famous *Mercury* are also displayed.

The Badia — This Benedictine church was founded in the 10th century by Countess Willa, mother of Ugo, the Margrave of Tuscany. It was enlarged in 1285 — the outer wing dates from this time — and then completely remodeled into a Baroque building by Matteo Segaloni in the 1620s. Over the elaborate *portal* (by Benedetto da Rovezzano, 1495) is a glazed terracotta lunette of the *Virgin and Child* by Benedetto Buglioni (15th century). Benedetto da Rovezzano also designed the Corinthian portico and vestibule to the church.
From the portico you get a fine view of the 14th century belltower whose lower section is Romanesque and upper section Gothic.

The interior, in the shape of Greek cross, is dominated by an incredible Baroque *ceiling.* Designed by Matteo Segaloni in 1625, the ceiling was carved by Felice Gamberai and Domenico Dotti. Major Renaissance works are to be found here. To the right is the *wall tomb of Giannozzo Pandolfini* (workshop of Bernardo Rossellini); by it is a bas-relief sculpted by Mino da Fiesole (1464-1469) as an altarfront with the *Virgin and Child blessing with Sts. Lawrence and Leonard.* In the right transept is the *tomb of Bernardo Giugni* by Mino (c. 1468) and, in the left one, Mino's masterpiece, the beautifully carved, *tomb of Ugo, Margrave of Tuscany* (1469-1481). Above the tomb is a painting of the *Assumption* by Vasari. The next chapel is frescoed with *scenes of the Passion* traditionally attributed to Buffalmacco, but actually by an unknown follower of Giotto. Just to the left of the church entrance is one of Filippino Lippi's finest works, the *Virgin appearing to St. Bernard* (1480). To the right of the choir is a door leading to the 15th century *Chiostro degli Aranci* (Cloister of the Orange Trees), a lovely two storey loggia. In the upper level are interesting frescoes of the *story of St. Benedict* attributed to the Portuguese painter, Consalvo.

Opposite the church is Via Ghibellina, with the Bargello on the righthand corner. Via Ghibellina 70 is the Casa Buonarroti.

The Casa Buonarroti (Michelangelo's House) — Purchased by Michelangelo, the house was made into a museum honoring him by his heirs. In the ground floor room are youthful works by the master, including a famous relief of the *Battle of Centaurs and Lapiths* and a *Virgin and Child* known as the *"Madonna di San Lorenzo."* There is also an original *bronze portrait bust of Michelangelo* by Daniele da Volterra. The adjoining room has a display of drawings, studies of nudes, portraits, and architectural designs. Also on the ground floor are casts of Michelangelo's statues preserved outside Florence, such as the Louvre Slaves, the Bruges Madonna, the Moses in San Pietro in Vincoli in Rome, the Rondanini *Pietà* in Milan, and others. Elsewhere in the museum are two other *portraits of the artist,* one by Bugiardini and one by Venusti, and a *portrait of Vittoria Colonna,* Michelangelo's closest friend.

139

Opposite Casa Buonarroti is Via delle Pinzochere which leads directly into Piazza Santa Croce.

Piazza Santa Croce — This square, more then any other in the city, has been witness to the changing lifestyles of the Florentine people. Here, early in the city's history, the people assembled to listen to preachers recounting the Gospel, here in the 15th century they came to watch the jousting matches of the royal knights (an unforgettable joust won by Giuliano de' Medici was even immortalized in verse by Poliziano), here throughout the 16th century they cheered for their favorite football teams, and so on, up to this day. One side of the square is bounded by the church, the others by old buildings, the two most interesting of which are No. 1, **Palazzo Cocchi-Serristori,** designed by Baccio d'Agnolo in 1470 and No. 21, **Palazzo dell'Antella,** built by Giulio Parigi in 1617. The striking façade of the latter is covered with frescoes painted in only 27 days by a team of 12 painters under the supervision of Giovanni da San Giovanni.

THE CHURCH OF SANTA CROCE — This church, which is one of the foremost Franciscan churches in Italy, rises on the site of a much more modest church, also Franciscan, which once stood here. Building of the huge basilica went on from the second half of the 13th century through the end of the 14th century. The result is a masterpiece of Tuscan Gothic architecture, often attributed to the genius of Arnolfo di Cambio, the architect who designed Palazzo Vecchio and the Cathedral. The marble façade is a modern 19th century work (1857-1863) by Niccolò Matas. The Virgin above the central portal and the Triumph of the Cross in the lunette below are by Giovanni Duprè. The Finding of the True Cross in the lefthand portal lunette is by Tito Sarrocchi, while the Vision of Constantine on the opposite side is by Zocchi. The graceful belfry designed by Gaetano Baccani in 1865 was inspired by the Gothic style.

From the beginning, there were Florentines for whom St. Francis' teachings of humility, poverty, and chastity—in contrast to what the majority of the day practiced — had great appeal. These early followers of the saint chose Santa Croce as their burial place. In fact, like Westminister Abbey in England, the church was soon filled with the tombs of noble Florentines and Florentine notables. The funerary monuments, tombslabs, plaques, and the like, grew in number over the centuries and made the church into a kind of local shrine. Thereafter it became a national shrine as scores of men, renowned in every branch of human endeavor, were laid to rest or honored with commemorative monuments in Santa Croce.

THE INTERIOR — The impressive church is in the shape of an Egyptian cross with Gothic-style pointed arches resting on elegant pillars along the nave. The ceiling, as the ceilings of all Franciscan churches, is of wooden beams. The walls were entirely covered with frescoes by Giotto up until the 16th century when Vasari was commissioned by Cosimo I to "modernize" the interior. This he did by whitewashing over most of Giotto's priceless 14th century frescoes and covering them with mediocre ones of his own invention. Starting from the inside of the façade we see the *monument to Gino Capponi* (the historian) by A. Bertone (1884) and the *monument to G. B. Niccolini* (the poet) by Pio Fedi (1883).
By the third righthand pillar of the nave is Benedetto da Maiano's exquisite *marble pulpit with the story of St. Francis* (1476).

RIGHT AISLE — By the first pillar is Antonio Rossellino's charming *Madonna del Latte* (Virgin of the Milk) of 1478. Opposite is *Michelangelo's Tomb* by Vasari (1564). Beyond the 2nd altar is the *Centotaph of Dante* (who however is buried in Ravenna) by Ricci (1839), beyond the 3rd altar Canova's neo-Classical *monument to Vittorio Alfieri* (the writer) and beyond the 4th altar is a *monument to Niccolò Machiavelli,* by Innocenzo Spinazzi (1787). To the left of the 5th altar and the *tomb of Luigi Lanzi* (the historian) by Giuseppe Belli (1810) is an exquisite Renaissance tabernacle framing a relief of the *Annunciation,* of *pietra serena*. It ranks as one of Donatello's finest works (1435). Just beyond the door leading into the cloister is another landmark

Basilica of Santa Croce.

of Renaissance sculpture, indeed the prototype of all Renaissance wall monuments, the *tomb of Leonardo Bruni* (the famed humanist and chancellor of the Republic). It is the masterpiece of Bernardo Rossellino (mid 15th century). Next is the *tomb of Rossini* (the composer) by Giuseppe Cassioli (1886). Rossini died in Paris in 1868 and eighteen years later his body was brought here.

Beyond the last altar is the *tomb of Ugo Foscolo* (the poet) with a statue by Antonio Berti (1939).

RIGHT TRANSEPT – On the extreme right is the **Cappella Castellani** (or *Cappella del Sacramento*) decorated with a 14th century fresco cycle by Agnolo Gaddi and Gherardo Starnina, among others. On the right are the *stories of St. Nicholas of Bari* and *St. John the Baptist,* while the *lives of St. John the Evangelist* and *St. Anthony Abbot* are recounted on the left. The painted wooden *crucifix* is by Niccolò Gerini (1386). The pillar statues of *St. Francis* and *St. Dominic* are della Robbia terracottas. At the end of the transept is the **Cappella Baroncelli** decorated with Taddeo Gaddi's marvelous fresco cycle illustrating the *life of Mary* (1338). Although the *Coronation*

141

Santa Croce - The interior combines the elegance of slender pillars separating the nave from the aisles and the simplicity of the Franciscan plan topped by a beamed ceiling. Along the walls are funeral monuments and tombs of famous men.

of the Virgin on the altar bears the signature of Giotto, it is probably a workshop piece. The painting of the *Virgin handing her girdle to St. Thomas* is by Sebastiano Mainardi (c. 1490). Outside the chapel, on the righthand side, is the *tomb of a member of the Baroncelli family* attributed to Giovanni di Balduccio of Siena (14th century). Next is a doorway which leads to a barrel-vaulted corridor, both of which were designed by Michelozzo. The door on the left leads to the 14th century **sacristy** decorated with frescoes of *stories of the Passion* attributed to Niccolò di Piero Gerini (late 14th century). The exquisite inlaid cabinets by Giovanni di Michele (1454) and Nanni Ungaro (1530) contain priceless illuminated missal books, ecclesiastical fittings, and relics of St. Francis. A Gothic wrought-iron gate closes off the **Rinuccini Chapel,** frescoed with the *stories of the Virgin and Mary Magdalen* by Giovanni da Milano and helpers (1366). The altarpiece of the *Virgin surrounded by saints* is by Giovanni del Biondo (1379).

142

Reentering the corridor, we go left until reaching the **Cappella dei Medici,** also designed by Michelozzo (1434). It contains a fine tabernacle by Mino da Fiesole (1474), a bas-relief attributed to Donatello, and, on the altar, a superb glazed terracotta, by Andrea della Robbia of the *Virgin and Child with saints* (c. 1480).

THE CHAPELS OF THE EAST END — The eleven chapels along the east end of the church were commissioned by the foremost Florentine families. Each one is named after its donor and consecrated to the family's patron saint. Starting from the right, the 1st chapel is the **Cappella Velluti** (which later passed into the hands of the Morelli and Riccardi families) bearing traces of frescoes of the *story of St. Michael the Archangel* by a pupil of Cimabue. The 2nd chapel, the **Cappella dei Bellacci,** frescoed by Taddeo Gaddi, was repainted by Gherardo Silvani in the 17th century. The 3rd, the **Cappella dei Silvestri,** later **Cappella Bonaparte,** contains a *monument*

Santa Croce - Tomb of Michelangelo.

to Charlotte Bonaparte by Lorenzo Bartolini. The 4th is the **Cappella Peruzzi** with a major fresco cycle painted by Giotto after 1320 that was whitewashed over, and then brought back to light and poorly restored — and repainted — in the mid 1800s (it was cleaned and restored again in 1959). On the righthand wall are *scenes from the life of St. John the Evangelist.* Starting from the upper register they are the *Vision at Patmos,* the *Raising of Drusiana,* and *St. John ascends to Heaven.* On the left wall are *scenes from the life of St. John the Baptist.* From above: *Zacharias and the Angel,* the *birth of St. John,* and *Herod's feast with Salome presenting the head of the Baptist.*

By the windows are figures of *saints,* while the four *Evangelists* are represented on the ceiling. The 5th chapel is the famous **Cappella Bardi** in which Giotto painted a fresco cycle on the *life of St. Francis.* The frescoes were recovered in 1853 and restored a bit more skillfully than those in the Peruzzi Chapel. Outside the chapel are *St. Francis receiving the Stigmata* and two medallions of *Adam* and *Eve.*

On the left wall starting from the top: *St. Francis giving up his worldly possessions, the saint appearing to St. Anthony preaching in Arles,* and the *death of St. Francis.* Opposite, from the top: *St. Francis giving the Rule to the order, being tried by fire before the Sultan,* and *Visions of the monk Agostino and Bishop Guido.* In the vaults are allegorical figures of *Poverty, Obedience, Chastity,* and *St. Francis in Glory.* On

144

Santa Croce - Monument to Dante.

the far wall are *Sts. Louis of Toulouse, Elizabeth, and Clair*. The *altarpiece* also relating the life of St. Francis is attributed to a painter from Lucca, Bonaventura Berlinghieri, a contemporary of the Saint (end of the 13th century). The **Main Chapel** (or **Cappella Alberti**) was frescoed by Agnolo Gaddi with the *Legend of the True Cross* (1380). Gaddi's lively narrative style served as a prototype for Florentine Gothic painting. The *altarpiece with the Virgin and Child* is by Niccolò Gerini. The four *Fathers of the Church* are by Nardo di Cione. The great *crucifix* is from the school of Giotto. The 7th chapel, the **Cappella Tosinghi** (later Spinelli and then Sloane), was once frescoed by Giotto. Of the original Life of Mary cycle only the *Assumption* on the outer arch is extant. The *altarpiece* is by Giovanni del Biondo (1372). — The *Pietà* in the 8th chapel, the **Cappella Capponi,** is a monument to the mothers of Italy. It was sculpted by Andreotti (1926). — The 9th, the **Cappella Ricasoli** has 19th century frescoes and paintings by Luigi, Giuseppe, and Francesco Sebastelli. The 10th, the **Cappella Pulci** (later Berardi and then Bardi) was frescoed by Bernardo Daddi (1330), the painter who successfully blended the monumentality of Giotto and the decorativeness of the Sienese school, and helpers. The subjects of the frescoes are the *Martyrdom of St. Lawrence* and the *Martyrdom of St. Stephen*. The ceramic *altarpiece of the Virgin and saints* is by Giovanni della Robbia. The 11th, the **Cappella Bardi di Vernio,** was frescoed by Giotto's favorite pupil, Maso di Bando, known as Giottino, with the

145

Santa Croce - *Above:* **Funeral of St. Francis by Giotto;** *left:*
the Bardi Chapel.

story of St. Silvester. The *altarpiece with the story of St. John Gualberto* was painted
by Jacopo di Cione at the end of the 14th century. — The chapel at the end of the
transept, the **Cappella Niccolini,** is a Baroque chapel designed by G. B. Dosio. In
the next chapel, another **Cappella Bardi,** is the famous wooden *crucifix* by Donatello
(c. 1425) which Brunelleschi harshly criticized as too realistic. To prove his point,
Brunelleschi then proceeded to carve a crucifix of his own, still hanging in the church
of Santa Maria Novella. On the left wall of the next chapel, the **Cappella Salviati,**
is a striking wall tomb by Lorenzo Bartolini (1837).

LEFT AISLE — Between the sixth altar and the door is the *tomb of Carlo Marsuppini,*
the famous humanist. Desiderio da Settignano, who sculpted this magnificent piece
around 1460, was inspired by the equally magnificent tomb carved by his teacher,
Rossellino, across the way. By the fifth altar are the *tombslabs of Lorenzo and his
son, Vittorio Ghiberti.* Between the first and second altars is the *tomb of Galileo
Galilei* by G. B. Foggini and G. Ticciati (1737).

147

Santa Croce - Pazzi Chapel.

THE PAZZI CHAPEL — The doorway just to the right of the church façade leads to a charming 14th century **cloister** whose leftside portico is actually the south church wall. On the far side is what many consider the epitome of Early Renaissance architecture, the Pazzi Chapel. This masterpiece of harmonious design was created by Brunelleschi between 1430 and 1446.

148

Outside, on the elegant portico, is a frieze of small medallions with cherub heads by Desiderio da Settignano. The portico is broken up by a barrel-vaulted arch, inside of which is a tiny hemispherical dome with terracotta decorations by Luca della Robbia. Luca is also responsible for the St. Andrew above Giuliano da Maiano's beautiful carved portal (1472). The interior, simple and of perfect proportions, reveals Brunelleschi's typical use of grey *pietra serena* stone against white plaster. The only color accents come from the frieze decorated with glazed terracotta motifs by Luca della Robbia, the medallions on the walls and in the dome pendentives of the *Apostles*, also by Luca della Robbia, and the stained glass windows of the apse designed by Alessio Baldovinetti. We turn left as we leave the Pazzi Chapel until reaching a doorway leading to a simple, harmonious **cloister,** another of Brunelleschi's designs.

The Santa Croce Museum — This small but important museum occupies rooms belonging to the church. In the largest, the former refectory, is a huge *Last Supper* fresco by Taddeo Gaddi.

The refectory also contains other noteworthy pieces such as Donatello's gilded bronze *statue of St. Louis of Toulouse* (c. 1425) originally made for Orsanmichele; Cimabue's great *crucifix* (back from years of painstaking restoration after being practically totally destroyed in the disastrous 1966 flood), *Sts. John the Baptist and Francis,* frescoes by Domenico Veneziano (1455), the remains of Andrea Orcagna's *Triumph of Death* and *Hell* (formerly in the church), and a *Virgin* by Bernardo Daddi. Sculptures of the 14th-16th centuries, including some by Tino di Camaino, are to be found in the nearby exposition halls.

Leaving Santa Croce, we turn left into Via Magliabechi. Along the left side of the street is the west wing of the **Biblioteca Nazionale** (State Library) which is entered from Piazza Cavalleggeri. The building, designed by Cesare Bazzini, was erected between 1911 and 1935. This world famous library, Italy's most important, contains priceless collections of old manuscripts and historical documents. At the end of Corso Tintori, the street intersecting Via Magliabechi, we make a left into Via de' Benci. The first building on the left side, number 6, is **Palazzo degli Alberti e dei Corsi** attributed to Giuliano da Sangallo.

The inner courtyard, designed by Giuliano da Sangallo presumably with the help of Andrea Sansovino, is particularly noteworthy. The building is presently the headquarters of the Horne Foundation.

The Horne Museum — The museum was founded by an English art connoisseur, Herbert Percy Horne. When he died in 1916 he left the mansion and his precious art collection to the City of Florence. The collection includes paintings, sculpture, *objets d'art,* furniture, hangings, and countless others. Two of the most interesting pieces on the ground floor are a 15th century *hopechest panel depicting Paris reclining* and an *Adoration* by Lorenzo di Credi. The outstanding paintings of the second floor include a *Virgin and Child* and a *Pietà* by Simone Martini, a *Deposition* by Benozzo Gozzoli, *Saints* by Sassetta, *Allegory of Music* by Dosso Dossi, *St. Jerome* by Piero di Cosimo, a fragment of an altarpiece by Pietro Lorenzetti, a *crucifix* by Bernardo Daddi, *Esther* by Filippino Lippi, and a *St. Stephen* attributed to Giotto. Among the sculptures the most interesting are a *wooden statue of St. Paul* by Vecchietta and a *bust of St. John* by a follower of Desiderio da Settignano. On the top floor are the prints and drawing collections, the library, as well as other art works.

Continuing down Via dei Benci towards the Arno we come to the reconstructed bridge known as Ponte alle Grazie. It has the same name as the bridge, destroyed during World War II, which stood near an oratory built by Jacopo degli Uberti in the 14th century to the *Madonna delle Grazie* (Our Lady of the Favors) on the right bank of the Arno. — After crossing the bridge, we continue a few yards in the same direction to Piazza Mozzi. Number 1 is the Bardini Museum.

The Bardini Museum — The museum was bequeathed to the City of Florence by a Florentine antique dealer, Stefano Bardini, in 1923. The windows of the rather odd-looking mansion are actually altars taken from a church in Pistoia. The collection, spread out over twenty rooms, covers many periods ranging from Etruscan, Greek, Roman, and 14th-15th century Italian sculpture, to paintings, tapestries, carpets, and furniture, mainly of the Renaissance period. The sculpture highlights of the collection are an *archaic Etruscan stone marker* (2nd century B.C.), a fragmentary *altar* with Bacchus and Maenads (Greek, 4th century B.C.), an allegorical *statue of Charity* attributed to Tino di Camaino, an altar base by Michelozzo, an altar frontal by Andrea della Robbia, and a terracotta *Virgin* (15th century Sienese school).

149

SEVENTH ITINERARY

Viale dei Colli - Piazzale Michelangelo - Church of San Salvator al Monte - Church of San Miniato al Monte - Viale Galileo - Via San Leonardo - Forte Belvedere.

Viale dei Colli — Once you have been inside the museums and churches of Florence, you are ready for a lovely drive along the Viale dei Colli. This winding, tree-shaded avenue which skirts the southern hills that encircle the city for over four miles, affords breathtaking views of the superb Tuscan countryside with the city of Florence as a backdrop. It is rightly one of the most famous drives in Italy. Starting from Piazza Francesco Ferrucci, we take Viale Michelangelo, which gently curves amidst the landscaped parks of villas and mansions, until we come to Piazzale Michelangelo.

PIAZZALE MICHELANGELO — The nicest place to stop along the scenic Viale dei Colli drive is Piazzale Michelangelo.
Its panoramic terrace commands an unforgettable view of Florence, her monuments, her river, her hills.

In the background, to the left is a big green zone, the Cascine Park. Towards the right is the triple peak of Monte Morello, immediately followed by the hills of Careggi, Montughi, and Pratolino. Practically opposite us, beyond the valley of Monte Senario, are the hills of Fiesole — the belltower of the Cathedral may be easily picked out in the middle. Continuing to the right, our glance encounters Monte Ceceri and immediately after, the castles dotting the Gerardo, Vincigliato, and Poggio hills, coming to rest on the hill of Settignano. From our vantage point, we can see all of Florence's monuments like doll houses below our feet. On the far left (this side of the river) we can make out the belltower of Santo Spirito and the characteristic dome of the Cestello Church. Across the river is the belltower of Santa Maria Novella, while closer to us, we can see the unmistakable tower of Palazzo Vecchio. Farther back is the marvelous complex of the Cathedral topped by Brunelleschi's dome and Giotto's belltower which dwarf the white-capped Baptistry beside it and the dome of the Medici Chapels of San Lorenzo in back of it. In front of Giotto's belltower we can make out the tower of the Badia Church with its pointed cusp. The Bargello's tower soars just to the right of the Badia, and still moving our eyes right we see the belltower of Santa Croce. The green dome not far away is the weathered copper dome of the Synagogue. Turning to the bridges spanning the river, we shall start from the one closest to us, Ponte alle Grazie, and continue left. The next bridge, Ponte Vecchio is unmistakable; it is followed by Ponte Santa Trinita, Ponte alla Carraia, Ponte Vespucci, with Ponte alla Vittoria in the distance. To our right is Ponte San Niccolò. Just below the terrace we are standing on is a massive tower-like structure. It is the San Niccolò Gate, built in 1324 after a design by Andrea Orcagna and was one of the defense points in the city walls protecting the medieval city. In the middle of the square we are standing in is a monument to Michelangelo (1875) whose genius is commemorated by copies of five of his best-known sculptures, the David and Dusk, Dawn, Day, and Night from the Medici Tombs in San Lorenzo. The monument and the layout of the Piazzale were conceived by

Church of San Miniato al Monte.

Giuseppe Poggi in the late 19th century. An inscription on the wall behind the little landscaped garden reads: "Giuseppe Poggi — Florentine architect — look around — this is his monument." On the hill behind Piazzale Michelangelo is the church of San Salvatore al Monte hidden among the cypress trees. It can be reached either on foot (staircase from Viale Galileo) or by car (turn left a bit beyond the terrace beneath San Miniato al Monte).

San Salvatore al Monte — Cronaca designed this simple church which Michelangelo called "the pretty country maid," in praise of its beauty — a fitting tribute to Cronaca's last work. His design is pure Renaissance: the interior is aisleless and elegantly plain, the ceiling beamed, and the apse rectangular. Several of the paintings decorating the altars date from the 15th and 16th centuries.

We reach the church of San Miniato perched on the hilltop by crossing the pleasant little park between San Salvatore and San Miniato.

THE CHURCH OF SAN MINIATO AL MONTE — From the top of the great stairway you can view all of Florence and the surrounding hills spread out beneath your feet. The church itself, begun in the 11th century and finished in the 13th, like the Baptistry, is one of the very few examples of Florentine Romanesque architecture extant. The upper section, with the green and white marble facing

San Miniato al Monte - Interior.

typical of the style — it was built in 1062 — is decorated with a 12th century mosaic of unknown authorship representing *Christ between the Virgin and St. Minias*. The whole is topped by a gilded bronze eagle symbol of the *"Arte di Calimala"* (the Woolmakers' Guild).

The interior is in the Romanesque style: it has a raised choir and correspondingly lowered crypt and a beamed ceiling. In the nave is an extraordinary marble floor with animal motifs and the signs of the zodiac (1207). All along the walls are traces of 14th century frescoes. In the middle of the nave is a free-standing tabernacle, the **Cappella del Crocifisso.** This masterpiece of Early Renaissance design was created by Michelozzo (1448), commissioned by Piero de' Medici (called Piero the Gouty) as a reliquary for the miraculous Cross of St. John Gualberto (now in Santa Trinita). The enamel decoration on the inner part of the tabernacle, by Luca della Robbia, is contemporary with the rest, whereas the paintings by Agnolo Gaddi are much earlier (1394). The subjects of the paintings are: *St. Minias and St. John Gualberto, the Annunciation and the Passion*. Behind the tabernacle are the stairs leading down to the crypt. The altar and columns belong to the original 11th century structure, while the beautiful wrought-iron gate dates from 1338. From the right aisle we take the stairway to the raised choir directly above the crypt. The fresco on the wall of the right aisle of the *Virgin and saints* is by Paolo Schiavo (1426). The choir is closed off by a superb *marble transenna* (screen) *and pulpit*. This unique work of 1207 is one of the foremost examples of Tuscan Romanesque sculpture extant. The inlaid choir stalls

153

Forte Belvedere.

date from 1466. On the 12th century main altar is a terracotta *Crucifixion* by the della Robbias. Along the lower section of the semicircular apse is black marble arcading, while on top are windows with pink alabaster panes. The striking apse mosaic of *Christ between the Virgin and St. Minias* dates from 1297.

To the right of the choir is a door leading to the **sacristy** (1387), entirely frescoed with sixteen very interesting *scenes from the life of St. Benedict* by Spinello Aretino. The furnishings are 15th century. — In the left aisle is a famous Renaissance monument, the so-called **Cappella del Cardinale di Portogallo** (the Chapel of the Cardinal of Portugal). It was designed (1459-1466) by a pupil of Brunelleschi's, Antonio Manetti, who was commissioned by King Alphonse of Portugal to create a fitting burial place for his nephew, Cardinal Jacopo di Lusitania, Archbiship of Lisbon, who had died in Florence in 1459. The five medallions in the ceiling showing the Cardinal Virtues and the Holy Ghost are by Luca della Robbia (1461-1466). In the righthand niche is the *tomb of the Cardinal* by Antonio Rossellino (1459-1461). The painting on the altar of *Sts. Vincent, James, and Eustachius,* is a copy of the original (now in the Uffizi) by Antonio and Piero Pollaiolo, while the *angels* frescoed on the niche are by Antonio Pollaiolo. Above the bishop's throne in the left niche is an *Annunciation* by Alessio Baldovinetti (1466-1467). At the end of the left aisle is the *tomb of Giuseppe Giusti* (the poet), with an epigraph composed by Gino Capponi.

The building to the right of the church, the **Palazzo dei Vescovi,** was put up in 1295 as a summer residence for the bishops of Florence. The belltower, built by Baccio d'Agnolo (early 16th century), was a prime target during the siege of Florence waged from 1527 to 1530. Michelangelo, who was put in charge of the defense of this zone, was thus compelled to stregthen his defenses by erecting an improvised fortress on the site of what is today the *Porte Sante Cemetery* to the right of the church.

Viale Galileo — Our scenic drive continues from Piazzale Michelangelo along the Viale dei Colli, here called Viale Galileo. On the left are charming villas set in landscaped parks. On the right are stretches of neat fields with the city as a superb background. The whole landscape is dotted with the tall dark-green cypress trees typical of the Tuscan countryside. About a mile from Piazzale Michelangelo we turn right into Via San Leonardo, a picturesque little country road which leads to Forte Belvedere.

If, however, we continue down Viale Galileo we soon come to Piazzale Galileo, the continuation of which is Viale Machiavelli, the last stretch of the Viale dei Colli. Viale Machiavelli winds its way through pleasant parks and gardens, descending to Porta Romana which, by way of Via Romana, leads us back into downtown Florence.

Via San Leonardo — This is one of the most charming country roads in the vicinity. Along the cobblestone road, you can see the grey-green olive trees peeping above the old stone walls and lovely villas, set in the typical Tuscan countryside of gently rolling hills. Halfway down, on the right, is a charming Romanesque church, **San Leonardo in Arcetri,** inside of which are 14th century Tuscan school paintings and a Romanesque *marble pulpit* (early 13th century). The road ends at Forte Belvedere. Continuing through the San Giorgio Gate (1324), a short walk downhill takes you back to the center of town.

Forte Belvedere — The building was erected between 1590 and 1595 by Giovanni de' Medici and Bernardo Buontalenti. Its ramparts command a superb view of the city below. Important art shows and other cultural events are periodically held here.

Via San Leonardo.

FIESOLE

This charming hilltown (c. 950 feet above sea level), a favorite jaunt with Florentines and sightseers alike, was originally settled by the Etruscans. The five mile drive to reach the town from Florence is an experience in itself — as we climb amidst splendid villas and country houses set in a superb Tuscan landscape of cypresses and olive groves, Florence appears beneath our gaze from a different position at every curve.

San Domenico of Fiesole — This picturesque town is halfway up the hill. It was named after the monastery of San Domenico erected here in the 15th century. The church on the main road has a 17th century façade by Matteo Nigetti. Inside are several fine paintings including a *Virgin and Child with saints* by Fra Angelico (who lived here before moving to the monastery of San Marco in Florence), a *Crucifixion* by followers of Botticelli, and others by Lorenzo di Credi, Sogliani, to mention only some. In the Chapter Room of the monastery is a *Crucifixion* by Fra Angelico (c. 1440).

Turning left opposite the church, a five minute walk takes us to the **church of the Badia Fiesolana** which was the cathedral of Fiesole until 1028. In 1466 it was rebuilt, along with the adjoining monastery, in the Brunelleschian style. The typically Romanesque green and white 12th century façade is set into a bare 15th century front that was never finished. The simple interior is harmonious and effective, reflecting the Brunelleschian influence. In the refectory of the monastery is a fresco of *Christ served by angels* by Giovanni da San Giovanni (1629).

Fiesole - Piazza Mino.

Returning to the main road, we continue our climb until reaching Piazza Mino da Fiesole, Fiesole's most important square.

Piazza Mino da Fiesole — The square is on the site of what was once the Forum. Opposite us, on the north side, are the Cathedral and, to the left, the **Bishop's Seminary.** On the east side, the building decorated with coats-of-arms is the **Palazzo Pretorio,** now the Town Hall, erected in the 14th century. To the right is an old chapel, the **Oratorio di Santa Maria Primerana,** extensively restored, with a 17th century façade. Inside the building are 14th century frescoes and other interesting works. The *equestrian monument* opposite the Town Hall representing the *encounter of the King of Italy, Vittorio Emanuele II, with Garibaldi at Teano* is by Oreste Calzolari (1905).

The Cathedral — Consecrated to St. Romulus, the building was begun in 1028 and later enlarged in 1256 and 1300. The whole building, façade, back, and sides, is made of plain stone, the effect of which is harmonious simplicity. The picturesque crenellated clock-belltower dates from 1213. The interior is typically Romanesque, with a raised choir and lowered crypt and a plain beamed ceiling. The columns along the nave came from Roman buildings. On the main altar is a *Virgin and Child with saints* by Neri di Bicci. The apse is frescoed with *scenes of the life of St. Romulus* by Nicodemo Ferrucci. To the right of the choir is the **Cappella Salutati** containing frescoes by Cosimo Rosselli (15th century) and two of Mino da Fiesole's finest works: the *tomb of Bishop*

157

Fiesole - *Above:* **Cathedral;** *below:* **Roman theater.**

Fiesole - Church of San Francesco.

Leonardo Salutati, with a bust of Salutati, and the *altar front with the Virgin and saints adoring the Child* (1464). The *altar and the statues of St. Romulus and St. Mathew* in the chapel to the left of the choir are by Andrea Ferrucci (1493).

The Roman Theater — You enter the archeological zone from the little road behind the apse of the Cathedral. In the **Faesulanum Museum** are objects excavated in digs carried out in this area. There are Etruscan tombs, architectural fragments, Etruscan and Latin inscriptions, coins, bronze, and even objects from the Barbarian period and late Middle Ages. Three of the highlights are an Etrusco-Greek statuette of *Hercules,* an Etruscan *mirror with the Sacrifice of Polyxena,* and a *portrait bust of the Emperor Claudius.*

The typically-Greek plan theater was discovered in 1809 and excavated in 1873. It was built at the time of Sulla, although it was later enlarged under Claudius and Septimius Severus (2nd-3rd century A.D.).
Clearly visible is the horseshoe-shaped auditorium with 19 rows of bleachers divided into three sections.
By way of the road going along the west side, we reach the *Etrusco-Roman temple.* On the right are the remains of an Etruscan gate and wall.

The Bandini Museum — The museum contains 15th-16th century della Robbia terracottas, as well as 14th-15th century paintings. The collection includes works by major artists, such as Ambrogio Lorenzetti, Nardo di Cione, etc.

The Church of San Francesco — To reach the church, you must take the little road by the Bishop's Palace. From the terrace at the top of the hill you get a breathtaking bird's eye view of Florence and the countryside spread out below your feet. There are some interesting paintings inside the Gothic-style church and the monastery contains a charming cloister and a Missionary Museum.

Finito di stampare
dalle Officine Grafiche Firenze
nell'Aprile 1979